Living
Free

Kristina Thomas

Cherisse,
May God bless
you richly on
your journey!
Love,
Kris

DEDICATION

This book is dedicated to the loving memory of

Eleanor Irvin
&
Lincoln Juillerat

Introduction

If you have gone through life without struggles, or never found it hard to find hope, consider yourself blessed beyond measure. But the truth is, many of us have endured struggles in varying degrees at some point in our journey. Depression, anxiety, loss of a loved one, low self-esteem, abuse, addictions and the list goes on. Unfortunately, many people stay on a treadmill of bad choices with one leading to another and then another because they haven't broken the chains that keep them bound; chains that keep one from living free.

I personally can speak to depression, loss and low self-worth, and how I was set free from those. But if an alcoholic said to me, "Yeah, but you don't know what it's like to be an alcoholic", they would be right. That's not a cross I've had to bear. It can be more difficult to connect and inspire someone if we have never sat in their seat or walked a mile in their shoes.

God has blessed me with collaborators for this book who have found freedom in surrender, all having had different chains broken in their lives. Each chapter is a stand-alone story of breaking chains and overcoming to live free. Our hope is that there will be one story in this book that you will be able to relate to if you are searching for freedom. One story that provides hope for another day, and the desire to break those chains that may be holding you back from fulfilling your purpose. If you are already living free, then we hope the stories inspire you to stay on your path and may possibly provide a nugget of truth to encourage you, or allow you to encourage someone else.

The devil comes to kill, steal and destroy. Those who find their redemption and make beauty for ashes are then able to share with others who are suffering and provide that glimmer of hope. As a society we love those Good vs. Evil movies. It's in the plot of just about every movie that has gained success; Star Wars, Narnia, The Wizard of Oz and the list goes on. We are fully aware that good and evil both exist and we want to see the good win out. In real life however, we often want to dismiss evil and hell, choosing to try and live happy and free on our own. When we have trials and tribulations we blame God instead of seeing it's the evil and sin that is alive and well in the world we live in. But we are here to give you hope – Jesus has overcome the world!! And in Him, you have the power to take back control of your life and Live Free!

"They triumphed over him by the blood of the Lamb and by the word of their testimony; they did not love their lives so much as to shrink from death." –
Revelation 12:11

CONTENTS

ACKNOWLEDGMENTS

Thank you to the following contributors for sharing their stories:
Denise Firth
Andrea Jordan Beasley – Author Ch. 1
Aaron White
Paige & Cody Jullierat
Jody Gulley

Thank you to Emmy Lee Jenkins for the cover photo and
Kensly Jett for additional photo edits

A sincere thanks to my special friends and family who supported and
encouraged me to keep pursuing this dream.
I love and appreciate each and every one of you!
And to my sons Matt & Jarred Carson who have always been my inspiration!

Preface

I have birthed the idea of writing a book in my heart for almost 30 years. Every time I would start I would find myself tripped up on things like "Who is my target audience? Fact or fiction? How do I even start?.." Those would be sudden bursts that would last a few days, maybe a week, as I would start to write. Those bursts would soon fizzle out with the busy life of a mom with two very active young boys.

In late 2013 when my boys were grown and I was on my own, the nudging to write once again started to consume me. While getting tripped up on the same things as before, I heard that still small voice say "Just write while you seek". To hold myself accountable, I posted the picture you will find on the back cover on my Facebook page and declared my vision: "This will be on the back cover of my book." Of course everyone wanted to know "What Book?" and at that time, I honestly didn't know. I only knew one day there would be one, and that day has arrived! Looking back I realized that it was never the right time before. 30 years ago I did not have the knowledge, wisdom and life experiences I have today. I had not been through the test, to give me the testimony. I had not yet met my amazing collaborators whose stories needed to be told.

One of my favorite verses in the bible is *"But seek ye first the kingdom of God, and his righteousness; and all these things shall be added unto you." Matthew 6:33.* When we get ourselves out of the way and stop trying to figure it all out, and instead get earnest in prayer surrendering it all to His will, it is added unto us. The right job, the right friends, the right opportunities. People often ask "I just wish I knew what His will was for me. How did you know?" I knew God placed a desire in my heart to write a book that would help others. But that's all I knew. I prayed daily "Put people in my path I can help and those who can help or teach me something." When I changed my focus and found freedom in surrender, things started to happen. People were put in my path at just the right time. That still small voice saying "Reach out in faith", and my being obedient. God has a purpose for each one of us, and when we seek Him above all else, that's when we find our purpose.

As I thought about writing this book I decided instead of trying to determine who my target audience would be, I would focus on the end result I wanted to achieve. The end goal? If the time and effort put into this book inspires or encourages just one person, God can use that one person to start a ripple that can change a lot of lives. I was blessed with collaborators who shared this same vision. If this book can offer hope to just one person, that one person could be the one to make a change in their corner of the world. If just one person reads a story and breaks the chains that bind them and finds the peace that a relationship with Jesus has given us; that peace that surpasses all understanding, even in the midst of mighty storms, then every moment spent writing was worth it and we will consider this a total success.

Thank you for picking up this book. Grab a cup of coffee, get comfortable, and our prayers are that as you read you will find a nugget of truth to encourage your soul.

CHAPTER 1
I'M NOT NORMAL

"I'm not normal". Those 3 words would consume my every thought, every minute of every day from the time I was a little girl until age 20. One of the first times I ever heard the tormenting voice was during one of my many showers a day as a child. As I sat on the floor of the tub, I almost heard it audibly. "What is wrong with you? Why couldn't you have just been normal. Something must be wrong with you for a grown man to want to touch you all of the time."

Every little girl who doesn't have a father around dreams of what it would be like if he were in her life. From the minute I was born, until age 6, having a father of any type was nonexistent for me. My biological father decided the responsibility of me was too much to bear at that time and chose not to have anything to do with me. Fortunately, the love of my mother and grandmother seemed to lessen the blow of that rejection. There were still times though, that I would find myself closing my eyes and putting myself in the role of being loved and parented by a male figure. And at the age of six the opportunity would arise when my mother would marry Eddie. Or so I thought.

It started months after the marriage, when Eddie would come into my room at night to molest me. I would wake up to a shadow at my door and pretend to be sleeping. My technique was to tuck my blanket underneath me as tight as possible, and to keep my arm between my legs. Some nights that would work, other nights he would pull the covers out from under me, unafraid of waking me.

Over time, Eddie became more confident in the location he would molest me and how often he would do it. It became an everyday thing, every time someone walked out of the room and we were left alone, even if only for a short time. He would find ways to get me alone; whether it was taking me to work with him, camping out, or what seemed to be his favorite, playing "games." As time went on he also became more comfortable with the things that he would do to me. As situations heightened with how Eddie would abuse me, so did my shame. I began showering up to three times a day, somehow trying to wash off whatever it was about me that made Eddie attracted to me. I remember wanting to just feel clean. It was in those multiple showers a day I would hear so clearly, "I'm not normal. What is wrong with me?" I didn't even want to be naked in the shower. I would cover up my body parts with rags so that I didn't have to see myself because I hated my body. I was so young I hadn't even had the chance to learn about who I was yet. I definitely didn't know anything about my sexuality, and I felt betrayed by my body that it was reacting without my permission.

I found out quick that the abuse was to be a secret. I was manipulated that if my mom found out, she would be devastated, and that was the last thing I wanted. Somehow at that point the shame shifted from him to me and the abuse became my problem. The burden of my mom not finding out wasn't his, but became mine as well. When the burden would become too heavy and he would see that I started to break down in front of my mom about not wanting to be around him, he would get a little more intense and speak vague threats about the repercussions of saying anything. Based off of other things I had seen in my home, I didn't doubt him. I feared him greatly.

When I was 9, Eddie's secret had been discovered when he abused my neighbor friend while she was at my house one day. By the time the cops had arrived he was gone and on the run from the law. I was relieved I didn't have to suffer the abuse anymore, but I was left to deal with the damage that had already been done. It was all over in my mind, I was going to stuff it down and leave it there and move on with my life; only I couldn't escape the deep roots in my heart of self-hatred, shame, and pain. Because of that, the abuse quickly became my identity, and followed me all throughout my teenage years.

For the next several years, I was able to stuff every feeling of the abuse far down to where I thought it couldn't touch me anymore. It was only a matter of time before the fruit of the root of abuse started to sprout in 7th grade. I would look at other girls in my class and wonder what it must feel like to be normal. I envied their care free attitudes and their worst problems only being a bad hair day. I wanted so desperately to be able to switch lives with them so that I could live my life normal. I felt trapped in a body that I was disgusted with and a mind that held shameful secrets. I knew who I truly was on the inside and I hated myself; and I knew if anyone else knew who I truly was, they would feel the same way about me as I did. I didn't even realize it, but I started conforming to the people around me and I learned how to act, talk, and walk like they did. Years of pretending, I became pretty good at hiding who I was to others. However, trying to convince others I was normal, while trying to figure out why I wasn't normal, became overwhelming to me and I started to feel depressed and severely anxious. The more I lost sight of myself the more my depression deepened and worsened, to the point of becoming suicidal my sophomore year.

After my teacher found a journal I had written, that expressed my desire to die, I was asked to see my high school counselor. Around the same time that I started counseling, I began medication through the psychiatrist. That's when the labels started; Depression, Anxiety Disorder. I started on anxiety medication and an anti-depressant. My depression only seemed to worsen with the medicine and I had to quit my job due to meltdowns at work. I couldn't concentrate in school and honestly didn't believe I would make it out of high school alive, so I fell behind in my grades. By the time I was a junior in high school I had tried a couple different medications for depression, but still none seemed to help, so I began drinking heavily. Any chance I could drink I would, and I never drank for anything less than black out. I did not want to be in reality anymore. I could never drink to the point of not remembering so I started mixing other things in with the alcohol. I experimented around with different drugs for a while, but still found no relief. I was spiraling out of control, and with every day that came, my mind became more and more tormented.

One morning I was called to the office to attend one of my counseling sessions at school. I had fought against seeing Mrs. Barnes for a long time before I finally gave in. Over time she proved herself to me as being trustworthy, and I began to open up. We dealt mostly with the fruit of all that was going on in my life based off the root of being abused. I wasn't ready to deal with the abuse quite yet, but she kept me going and kept sparking up hope in me with every session. The hope didn't come from her telling me a list of things to do, or what not to do. It didn't come from her telling me to try this med or that med to cover up my pain, but she would talk to me about **God**. I had a foundation of God and loved Him so much as a child, but had lost sight of Him through all life had brought my way. I was confused how He could love me and care about me, and yet let people hurt me so bad. I was convinced He was the author of my pain. Still, somewhere *deep* inside of me I felt like He was the way out of my misery, I just couldn't see how. It was in that session when I was 17 years old that I expressed to Mrs. Barnes that maybe I needed to start attending church. I knew of one I had went to when I was younger, but I expressed my fear of going alone. She validated my feelings, but challenged me. "What is the worst thing that could happen if you were to go to church and sit alone?" I sat quiet for a minute and thought about it, and the worst thing I could come up with is that people would be looking at me sitting alone. With that realization, I decided I would push through the fear and go to church that Sunday.

Making a decision to go to church every Sunday was good for me. I believe it was the next step God had for me getting closer and closer to freedom in Him, but somehow I seemed to be continuing to get worse. By this time I had been on several different anti-depressants, anxiety medications, and sleeping pills. Suicide was constantly on my mind. In my mind, if church didn't fix me I didn't know what would. I had been staying with a family from the church I was attending and basically depending on them to keep me alive. I required a lot of attention. The problem was that I was looking for the attention of people who couldn't fill that void in my soul that I so desperately longed for. My identity crisis hit an all-time high and I learned quickly what would keep their attention on me, even if it meant lying about any and everything. With lying all of the time, came an immense amount of shame. I couldn't keep up with my lies. And with the unraveling of lies came the unraveling of an identity that I worked so hard to build up all of my life, to avoid the real me, who I hated so much.

I was unraveling and my past was catching up with me like never before. I wasn't ready to deal with me, so I began sleeping constantly. I would sometimes sleep until 6pm, wake up and smoke a cigarette, and go back to sleep for the night. My curtains, bedspread, and rugs in my room were all black. I was so dead on the inside. There were countless nights I would overmedicate myself with my meds or sleeping pills and beg God that He would take me when I went to sleep. I would wake up the next morning mad at God. I would hear about suicides in my area and read into every detail, secretly envying that they succeeded. I felt there was no other way out. I didn't even feel that *deep* feeling any longer that someday it could be better. It was only a matter of time before my life was over. What I didn't know was that God was working on my behalf for a way of escape, I just couldn't see it.

It was the summer of 2010. I had been out with a friend one night driving around for hours, which was the norm for us. We'd stop and get our cigarettes and pop, put in some music and have it blasting and just drive. This was a form of escape for my mind. We would mostly go on these road trips after midnight and get back at 2 or 3am, only this night God shook my world up a bit. Before she picked me up that evening I was lying in my bed flipping through the channels on the TV when I stopped on a woman singing. It was Cece Winans. "I've heard of her" I thought, as I continued listening. As I continued to watch she sat down with Nancy Alcorn, who began to talk about Mercy Ministries. She began telling testimony after testimony of girls who had dealt with the same things I was dealing with. She spoke of how they overcame sexual abuse and lived normal lives. She spoke of how they overcame depression and suicide and no longer dealt with it. They were free. She talked about how God transformed their entire lives and made them new. Something stirred within me as I thought to myself, "Is that really possible?" She continued speaking and listed off the homes and where they were located. The closest one to me was in Nashville. "Oh never mind, I can't leave my family and friends and move away for 6 months." I thought. At about that time my friend pulled up so I turned my TV off and left for a night of driving.

We got home in the middle of the night. My friend just decided since it was so late that she was going to stay the night with me. When we had settled in for the night we flipped through channels trying to find something to watch, and in time, fell asleep. When my friend woke up to leave in the morning for work, I got up and turned my TV on, only to see a re-run of the same program from the night before with Nancy talking about Mercy Ministries. I knew for a fact my friend and I had not been watching spiritual channels the night before. That's when God hit my heart with confirmation, that's where I was supposed to be. Still, I reasoned in my mind it was impossible. I felt hopeless and helpless, and oddly enough, I had become comfortable in my misery.

As summer came to an end, my torment was beyond anything it had ever been. Sitting outside one evening smoking, I felt completely numb. I had reached the point of absolutely feeling nothing for life. I looked up to the clouds and wept harder than ever before. I cried out to God, "I can't do this anymore God!! I'm in so much pain and I'm so tired!" With those words, I proceeded to put my cigarette out on my arm. I just remember being confused as to why I couldn't even feel the burn from my cigarette? In that confusion, I kept re-lighting it and putting it out again in my flesh. I continually did this until I ran out of room and then I switched arms. I picture my life at this point almost like a boxing match. I was getting hit over and over and over again, wavering back and forth, delusional and SO tired. It would take one more punch and I'd lose the fight. My enemy saw my weariness on September 28, 2010, and with anticipation, thinking he was about to win, he drew back for one last punch.

First thing, as soon as I opened my eyes that morning I could feel a darkness surrounding me so heavily. It overwhelmed me. It scared me. I grabbed my phone and quickly dialed the mother of the family who had been trying to help me. I begged her to come get me and bring me over to her house that night, because I was dependent on her keeping me alive. When she told me she wasn't able to have me over that night, in anger I threw my phone at the wall and it broke into pieces. I went outside to smoke and as I sat there my mind settled into an eerie comfortable place of numb. I can only describe it as feeling completely out of reality. I decided it sitting there, today was the day I was going to kill myself. I was done talking about it, and for a moment I felt relieved that it was going to be over soon. I got up and went upstairs to my room. This demonic calmness came over me as I pulled out multiple prescriptions from my purse. I poured every container out one at a time; Pain pills, muscle relaxers, sleeping pills, and anti-depressants. I sat on my bed surrounded in pills. Everything went silent. I wasn't thinking about my family, or friends. I wasn't thinking about who would find me, or how long it would take to die. I wasn't thinking at all, but what I *felt* was the pressure of heaven and hell waiting. I felt the devil himself and his demons in the corner of my room waiting, in anticipation. I was dangling over hell and it all came down to my decision. I looked over at my phone on the floor and something moved me to pick it up and put it back together. I truly don't know what my intentions were for that or what moved me to do that, but I put the battery back in, sat it down, and went back to my bed. I scooped the pills up into my hands and started crying as I brought them closer to my mouth. 13 years of feeling abnormal and tormented was finally coming to an end. I stood there waiting for the devils last punch to hit me and win; that's when Jesus in His Mercy, stepped in front of me to fight for me. At that exact moment my phone started to ring.

Startled as if someone had just barged in my room I dropped the pills. I got up and ran to my phone. I answered a teary voice screaming at me. "DON'T YOU EVER HANG UP ON ME AGAIN, DO YOU HEAR ME!?" I pleaded with her to just let me go. I expressed to her I just couldn't do it anymore and that I was done fighting. She begged and screamed for me to call my mom or she would call the police or my mom herself. She cried as she reassured me things could be better and not to take my own life. I hung up and called my mom to come get me. From there I was transported to the hospital where I was admitted to the Psychiatric Ward for 5 nights.

Being in the hospital really put things in perspective for me. Something had to give. It was time for change. If God wasn't going to let me die then I needed to know what the purpose was for me to continue to live. I didn't know where else to turn so I made a decision that I was going to apply to Mercy Ministries. In the process I had toured another girl's home and didn't feel like it was where I needed to be. I felt in my heart Mercy was where I needed to be. For months I would stay up all night on the Mercy website. Reading about their beliefs, about the founder, and what took up the most time; testimonies of girls who had been through the program. I would read some stories and think, "WOW that's just like my story!" It didn't fix all of my problems, but made me realize I wasn't alone. Other girls were dealing with the same things and coming out FREE. The application process took a while and then I would have to be accepted. Drs. Appointments, phone calls, check in calls, were all I did. I would set alarms to wake up and make a phone call. Sleep until a dr. appointment and go back to sleep. In my weakness, the Lord's strength took over to help me make it until I finally got accepted. I could have been on the waiting list for months, but a couple weeks after being accepted I received a call from the program director telling me to be there in 10 days.

I walked through the doors of Mercy Ministries May 16, 2011, and that was the day my life would forever change. That's where I met Jesus.

I would like to say shortly after I accepted Christ into my life at Mercy that my life was all wonderful and happy and my problems ended. Accepting Christ into my life was THE most important thing, and yes in Him I became a new person, but my mind didn't change. As a matter of fact it took several months before I even felt slightly better. I had spent 19 years with the mentality that I was not normal, and countless years of suicidal and depressing thoughts. It took some time of speaking scriptures and getting them into my soul before old mindsets started fading away. It took some "working through" memories of abuse and inviting the Lord into those hurtful places. Which usually led to countless nights of panic attacks on the bathroom floor, crying out to God with pain inside that I can't even put into words. It took some **time**. One big thing had changed though, I now had the Lord's help to make it through. The nights on the bathroom floor of Mercy, that's when I experienced God's character of comfort. Speaking scriptures out loud multiple times a day started showing me His supernatural power. Inviting Him into the hurtful places during counseling, and hearing what He had to say about where He was when I was being abused, dissolved all my anger towards Him. The more I experienced His perfect love towards me, the fear started leaving. God could have delivered me over night, because He's God and He holds the world in His hands, and I used to despise the fact it had to be a process of going through, but it was in those times though that He constantly came to my rescue that I learned He was trustworthy and reliable. Through the **process** I experienced the Truth of Who God is, and with that came wholeness, healing, peace, hope, and **purpose**. When I started to understand who I was in *Him*, I started healing, and the more I healed the more the medications started dying off. I realized I didn't need depression medication, because I found a joy that was unexplainable. The anxiety medicine I was on 3x a day I stopped taking because the fear started to leave. The anti-psychotic I took for bi-polar disorder actually started giving me anxiety because it was messing with my mental state. As the Lord started healing the memories of abuse I stopped taking sleeping pills at night because I was beginning to sleep peacefully for the first time in my life. All of the disorders and labels started to fall off of me and I became free; and it wasn't temporary, 3 1/2 years later and I'm still medication free.

The things the devil meant for my harm, God has turned for my good!! I'm able to relate to so many people who go through sexual abuse and the torment it leaves them in, and now spreading the Word that through Jesus they can be free too! I am an assistant in a "Living Free" ministry in my church; Counseling and teaching women the character of God and His love for them individually, and seeing lives transformed through the power of His Word. The Lord has restored the opportunity to get back into college and I'm currently enrolled to study theology. Through His love I've come to **love myself,** who He made and designed me to be. My purity was so important to me, and something I have always in my heart valued so much, and through the power of Jesus that has been restored to me! Life gets better every single day that I wake up. I have a hope when I wake up each morning, and it's the hope of experiencing the Lord on this earth just one more day. There is not one thing about me that desires death any longer. I love life. I love Jesus. And it's all because He first loved me.

Jesus gave my life **purpose**. And He is, with such love, awaiting the opportunity to reveal yours to you.

7/13/15

My sweet Jesus,

What have you done for me?? Too many things to even say. Words would never do you justice for the people. But I'll try. You became the Father to me that I have been searching for my entire life. I'm comforted in the fact that I have a Father to go to about any situation or circumstance. Earthly Fathers can give good gifts, but what you have done for me far surpasses them all. You have given me the gift of being yours. Being loved by you has been the foundation of what has set me free to be me. You have shown me what it is to be fearfully and wonderfully made. I had such a lost identity based off of things that had been done to me and things I had done, but you showed me who I was meant to be all along. The real me. You showed me how much the real me was valued in your eyes and how to find that little girl I had lost so long ago in abuse. The joyful, pure, innocent girl who found her purpose in being loved. You have filled every void. Finding out what you say about me and who I can be has given me hope. The supernatural things you've promised to deliver me from since day one have come to pass and you only continue to show how trustworthy you are day after day. You're a worthy God who is so worthy of our trust. Not one person who reads what you have done for me will ever have to wonder if it's possible when they accept you into their life. Because you cannot deny who you are. The only thing hindering us from full freedom in you is ourselves. You have given us this free gift that we're so undeserving of when you sent your Son Jesus to the Cross. We were made to know you, and to love you, and to believe in you. And until we find our identity in you and hear what you have to say about us we'll never find true fulfillment or peace. I'm blessed to have found that. I'm blessed to keep finding it. I'm still discovering who you originally intended for me to be day by day. Still discovering you and your heart and your character. And with every experience I fall more in love with you every day. Help the people reading this book to understand fully Jesus just how great you are and how much hope there is in your name alone.

Love,
Andrea

"Therefore if any man be in Christ, he is a new creature: old things are passed away; behold, all things are become new."
2 Corinthians 5:17

CHAPTER 2
CHAINS OF ALCOHOLISM

"Look at that window, you are two stories up. You can run and crash through it and fall to the ground and this will all be over. Isn't that what you want? Aren't you tired and ready to give up? Let's just end this, now! Hurry, before they come back in the room!" As she sat waiting for the Pastors to enter back into the room she found herself hearing those words in her head and wondering why? Why am I thinking those things? I have never had a suicidal thought in my life! Why now? It was the devil whispering in her ear, and his enemy was preparing to walk back into the room and remove him from her life...

"Mom, you need to leave the room and leave us alone with your daughter." the pastor said as she re-entered their office and kicked off her high heels getting ready for the task at hand. She and her husband were both Pastors and they were going to pray over this young mother until she was set free from the demons of alcoholism and addiction that were threatening to take everything from her that she once held dear.

Denise was raised in a loving home, attended a private Catholic school and did not suffer at the hands of any abuse or neglect, always feeling loved and protected. Denise always felt she had a treasure in her heart and would be used greatly someday. She knew God, but she kept Him at arm's length. She didn't want to feel any conviction, she wanted to have fun! At this time the legal drinking age was 18 years old. She wanted to drink and party and laugh with her friends, she would get serious about God, later. For now, there was fun to be had and she was going to be right in the middle of it with her infectious smile and bubbly personality.

Denise can recall attending a "Drink n' Drown" once at the age of 18, but for some reason, she elected not to drink that time. She just sat and watched everyone else get drunk and realized that she didn't want her entire life to be one big "Drink n' Drown". But for now she was good, she had control, she would only party for a time and then she would settle down and be the woman her mother kept telling her God had created her to be.

Denise's mother held bible studies in their home and was always encouraging Denise to attend. She prayed for Denise daily and wanted her to find the Lord. Instead, at the age of 19, Denise found 36 year old Frank. Frank was a rough and tough guy and was no stranger to violence. They got married and had two daughters. But their family life was far from perfect. Denise was still drinking and partying, they were going in debt further by the day, and their marriage suffered at the hands of mistakes made while intoxicated. She and Frank would argue and fight, and the more they fought, the more she drank.

It became evident to family members and friends that Denise may likely have a problem with alcohol. She told those who asked that she was fine and promised she would one day stop drinking. But instead, she just hid it. There were bottles of alcohol hid behind the commode and in the laundry so she could act the role of the good mother and wife, yet get her addiction fed in secret. Eventually she could not get through a day of work without a drink. The alcohol was hid behind filing cabinets and in desk drawers. She would come home and drink more passing out on the couch early. Her life revolved around that next drink, that next party or night out with her friends while she left Frank and the girls behind. The lies and deception and everything that comes with alcoholism caused her world to eventually come crashing down around her. Frank left and took the children with him. She moved into her mother's home where she tried to get better on her own, but just couldn't fight those demons that continued to whisper *"You need a drink. Just one more drink won't hurt you."*

Denise's brother called and said he had arranged for her to fly to California and be signed into the Betty Ford Clinic. She slowly and reluctantly packed her bags. As they got into the car and prepared to leave for the airport, her mother felt the urging to stop by the church on the way. That turned out to be the pivotal point in Denise's life. That one stop, that one moment in time and it changed everything. As she sat there in the Pastors office waiting on them to come back in the devil was trying to get her to end it, to put her soul in a continual hell for eternity. The voices in her head trying to convince her she was already living in hell and there was nothing better. But that's when the power of Jesus showed up in the hands of two pastors who prayed over her until she found victory! She felt herself going in and out as they prayed and she came to, feeling free for the first time in a long time. There was a peace in her soul she had not experienced in years; and with that peace, for the first time in a long time, a glimmer of hope.

The pastor gave good advice as she counseled Denise "You cannot worry about making it right with everyone today. You need to get yourself right first, with God. Once you have found your worth in your creator and start to seek Him, the rest will fall into place. If you reach out to those you have hurt right now, they will likely reject you and you will get discouraged. Build yourself up, be the new creature and God will restore to you what you have lost." She shared with her the following verse from Hebrews 11:6 – "But without faith it is impossible to please him: for he that cometh to God must believe that He is and that He is the rewarder of those who seek Him." She pressed Denise to diligently seek him first and he would then reward her, restoring all she had lost. As she will tell you, it's not an easy road. Everything doesn't just magically and instantly become OK. But God will give you the strength to keep pushing forward, to keep believing, to keep standing firm until you reach the other side of healed and whole and life is no longer what it once was.

As Denise went to walk out of the room she glanced down and saw the cigarettes lying in the top of her purse. She heard a voice say *"Oh those are OK, just keep those…"* She grabbed them up and gave them to the Pastor and said "No more! I'm free!" She knew she could not let the devil have one area of her life ever again. She had found freedom in surrender!

Authors note: I walked up to the church that bright sunny day and was greeted by a man in cowboy boots and a warm smile. He shook my hand and welcomed me to my new church. I remember thinking he had such a sweet spirit about him. I sat in the back of the church and watched as he later came in and sat down next to a beautiful woman.

She was poised and one of those women who just seemed to have it all together. During praise and worship they had their hands in the air and were praising God. The woman was full of energy and zeal and you could tell she had an intimate relationship with God. Over the following weeks I learned the young woman on stage singing was their daughter. That they raised horses on their farm and owned their own business. They were mighty prayer warriors and a couple who helped others in the church and headed the "Living Free" class. You often saw sweet, gentle Frank holding the babies during service. So imagine my surprise when the church played the "Redeemed" videos on the screen one Sunday morning as Easter approached. There was Denise's daughter on the screen talking about how Frank used to be a gangster and Denise an alcoholic. How their family was crumbling before her mom found the Lord. What?!? This couple?? And in that instant God spoke to my heart with the realization that we often see people on the good side of healed and whole and we become envious of the fire they seem to have in their soul. Envious of the amount of faith and strength they have. As humans we are too quick to judge and assume that they have just always had it like that. But the truth is this: many times the fire and faith you see in some people are because they were truly snatched out of the hands of hell, dangling at the edge of their existence, and given a new start. They know where they once were, where they are now, and they have much to praise God for! Once you hear of the tests and trials that brought their testimony, and see how they are living today, you are given hope that it can happen for you too!! God does still heal, still breaks chains, restores families and sets people free!!

"When the Lord brings you out into the light, you can never remember how dark it was." – TD Jakes

CHAPTER 3
ABUSE, ANGER & ADDICTION

"Look Mom! I know Him!"   Aaron's mom looked shocked as she turned around and saw Jesus on the television. The shock came from the fact that only a week prior Aaron had fell and broke his neck. That was the first time Aaron met Jesus. It would be 15 years before they met again...

My older brother and I lived with our mother and father during those early years. Dad was involved in motorcycle gangs and there was always alcohol and drugs in our home. Dad had a quick, hot temper and that would often afford my brother and I severe whippings.   An environment that should have been safe for a young boy was, instead, unpredictable and hostile. That caused feelings of being helpless and weak in the early formative years of my life. Over time those feelings of being weak and helpless would slowly turn into an anger that would eventually consume me.   In contrast to the physical and mental abuse, dad often told us to believe in God and Jesus. I always felt growing up that there was something "more" but wasn't exactly sure what that was. Hearing about God and Jesus, but not having the example in the home, made it hard for me to understand. In those early years I was a straight A and honor roll student who participated in school sports and had friends, yet I always felt empty inside, like something was missing. There was a longing in my soul that I didn't know how to fill. I started to experiment with things so readily found in our home, hoping they may fill the void that seemed to grow larger with each passing day. I smoked marijuana for the first time at age 11. The same age I also discovered pornography.

At the age of 13 things took a turn for the worse when dad suffered a heart attack. After the heart attack he lost his business and severe depression set in. That's when dad started taking valium and other prescription medicine. Taking the medication would cause him to become more volatile. With the increase of abuse against us by our father, we needed our mother more than ever. But then a day that is etched in my memory so vividly unfolded. Unable to withstand all she was enduring during that time in our lives, mom decided she needed to leave. Christmas morning we woke up and she was gone. We didn't know where she was as we walked up to the gas station in the middle of a cold snowstorm to use the phone and file a missing person's report. We soon found out that she had left us to go live with her boyfriend in the middle of the night. That event was very traumatic for young boys at such a critical, tender age. A divorce soon followed and as it came to an official close; my brother went to live with my mom and I chose to stay with dad. Even amidst the abuse and life style we had been living, I did not want to leave him alone.

During this time in my life I often thought of running away. I didn't know where I would go or how I would get there, but I knew there had to be someplace that was better than the life I was living. I was blessed to be able to spend a lot of time with my best friend and his family. I felt peaceful when I was with them. One summer they invited me to go to Destin, FL on vacation with their family. I remember waking up and looking at the clock. It was 3 a.m. and I was wide awake. I quietly slipped out of the room and started walking the beach, listening to the water quietly lap against the shore. I wanted so badly to just keep walking and never look back. The constant thought in my mind as I walked was just the overwhelming desire to start a new life; I just didn't know how or where to start. Eventually I went back to the hotel and as the vacation ended, back to my harsh reality. My friends' family offered to adopt me, that could have been my way out, yet I could not grasp ahold of that opportunity. I didn't want to hurt my parents, so I stayed in the lifestyle I was growing accustomed to.

Living with dad in an apartment in a neighborhood riddled with drugs and illicit behavior, the abuse started to get worse. As the abuse got worse at home, the anger and rage got worse inside. I found myself in my first fist fight at the age of 14, and sadly, it was with my father. I came home at 11:01 and my curfew was 11:00. As I was walking up to the apartment dad ran out of the apartment, met me in the front yard and started punching me. It was surreal that this was actually happening. When I was 14 mom decided that when I came to visit it would be OK for her to buy my cigarettes and smoke marijuana together. Everyone in my circle, young and old were doing some sort of drugs and it just became the norm for my existence.

Before my 15th birthday arrived, I was smoking weed every day. I had also started selling it as well. I sold to my parents, cousins and family. Selling drugs lead me to bad connections and acquaintances. The daily intake of marijuana caused me to lose any drive or desire I may have once had for school or sports. My straight A's and honor roll status started to become nothing but a distant memory. School was now a place to make money by selling drugs. I was 16 years old when my buddy introduced me to cocaine for the first time. I'd go re-up downtown, come back home and keep half for myself, and cut up the other half mixing with other things. I was only hooked on cocaine about 6 months when mom's boyfriend introduced me to pills. Nerve pills and pain meds soon became my drug of choice. Mom's neighbors and friends would give me their prescriptions, I'd go sell the pills and bring them back the money and they would let me keep some of the pills as payment. I could either take them or sell them. Eventually I found myself hooked on prescription drugs. While becoming a drug dealer, I also became known for my ability to fight. The rage still welled up in me and if I felt like someone was disrespecting or making fun of me, those feelings of rage from the childhood beatings and feeling helplessness would rise up inside. That pent up anger would be released on anyone crossing my path. I often had friends who would come calling wanting me to go fight other dealers who owed them money or drugs. The drugs became expensive and that's when I started to steal things to pay for my addiction. Every time a fight was over or an item was stolen, I started to feel the conviction in my heart, overwhelmed with sadness and remorse for who I had become. I didn't want to hurt anyone, didn't want to fight, but I was operating on auto pilot, in survival mode. I was living the hand I felt I had been dealt. There was no peace, no solace, just hurt and pain for the life I found myself living. Maybe there was still hope? I had not turned completely cold.....

My first felony came at 17 years old when I got busted for trafficking and narcotics. Undercover narcotics agents had been following me as I purchased Xanax bars from a man who would fly a plane to another country and return with the drugs. Only a TV, chair and piles of drugs were found in this man's apartment. I never did know the dealers name; I only went to handle the transactions. The introduction came from a young woman that I was buying off of when she offered to just introduce me directly. Because I was 17 when I was busted, I went to Juvenile detention for one month and that transferred into being under house arrest. I was also required to participate in a recovery center program for 6 months. It wasn't long until I quickly learned how to manipulate the system. I could still do drugs and smoke weed and drink enough water to get it all out of my system before being tested on Wednesdays. The counselor was a young girl who graduated from Ohio State. When I discovered she was from a middle class family and had never done drugs or had any idea where I was coming from, I shut down and had no respect for her. How could she possibly help me when she had no reference point for the things I had endured and the addictions I was struggling with?

After the arrest, I moved out of my father's apartment and started living with a buddy. I stopped going to regular school and went to "virtual school". By signing up for the work release program I was able to leave at 9:30 a.m. Sadly, my "work" was still being a drug dealer. I sold drugs to fellow students and to this day I still carry remorse and guilt for those I sold to that became addicted. Breaking into stores for stupid stuff also became part of my routine. We would be so strung out on drugs that if we didn't have cigarettes, we would just break into a store for a pack of cigarettes. There was no thought of consequence, just satisfying the need we had in the moment. We were living on the edge just doing what we could to make it from one high to the next.

The longing to escape and be normal never left me; there had to be more, the loneliness and torment in my heart was almost too much to bear. When the loneliness came, it would get chased away with another drug, another high. At 18 years old I tried to join the Marines. That could be my way out. I could serve my country, clean up my life, and find a way out of this lifestyle that had consumed me. My heart sank as they informed me that with a felony on my record, I could not be accepted into the Marines.

The pain pills became too expensive and that's when I was introduced to Heroin by an upstairs neighbor. I started doing Heroin at 19 because it was cheaper. At that time I was smoking black tar. While many get hooked that first try and cant' get off, I was able to go off heroin for a time and take the prescription drugs. Some heroin is weak, some strong. I found myself scared of the heroin because I never knew what it could potentially be laced with. The prescription pills like OxyContin, you knew what you were getting and how much you could handle. Many times the pills were stronger than the heroin. But by this point in my life, I had to have something every day just to feel "normal". Have you ever been in a conversation and had an awkward moment? That is how I felt all the time when being around people if I was not high. Being high was my normal. But yet I was still empty and lonely inside. I remember specifically a Halloween party I threw. I found myself standing shoulder to shoulder with other so called "friends" and yet I felt like I was totally alone at my own party. As a drug dealer I found my friends were only there when they needed something from me. There was no one I could truly count on to always be there.

Depression and thoughts of suicide were stronger than they had ever been. I felt like I was in a deep, dark hole that was swallowing me up with no way out. The depression started keeping me at home, alone. The phone rang, it was dad. He continued to call multiple times and left messages. It was a tradition to go to grandma's house on Christmas Day. Dad was trying to get ahold of me to see if I would go. Eventually dad showed up at my apartment. He knocked on the door and waited... knocked again... I just sat there on the couch in the darkness and didn't answer. I did not want grandma to see me this way. As dad walked back to his car I got up and looked out the window. As he started to drive away I opened my door and tried to yell after him, but it was too late. He was too far gone and I couldn't catch him. It was at that point that I had given up all hope and wanted to end it because I felt like I could never get back out of what I was in.

I was now going from job to job, changing about every 6 months, and had accepted that I was never going to be more than a drug dealer. I was technically homeless, although I never stayed on the streets. I would stay with whatever friend or family member would let me crash for a while. Eventually I would steal from them to support my habit and they would kick me out and I would look for somewhere else to stay. Even though I often thought of committing suicide at that point, I could never find the courage to go through with it. I finally made my way to my older sister's house, which would be my last stop.   I had a step-brother and step-sister that were older. My step- brother had been delivered from drugs and filled with the Holy Spirit. At the time when he was talking about that, I had no idea what that meant. When he turned his life around he moved out of state where he met and married a beautiful Christian woman and they started a family. My step-sister was living in town and married as well with a family. My staying there was starting to cause problems for my sister. Her husband gave her an ultimatum, it was him or me, but he could not let me stay with them anymore. Her heart was breaking and torn as she wanted to save me, her brother, but had her own family to consider.

One night as I was super high and walking back through my neighborhood with a backpack of stolen items and a pocket of money, I watched a church van pull in and stop up ahead of me. I had gotten to the point I was selling everything I owned; even valuable items that had sentimental memories for me. Jewelry worth $200, I would sell for $20. I had truly hit rock bottom. I was sleeping all day and up stealing stuff all night. I had reached the point something drastic was going to have to happen. I was likely either going to prison or get killed, or I had to find that escape, but how? To get back to my drug dealers house I would have to walk through this group of people who had stepped out of that church van. There were about 10 of them standing there. It was a "wall of Christians". They stopped me and asked my name. I don't recall much of the conversation, but what I do recall is someone saying "Can we pray for you?" I said "Yes" and as they prayed I felt such warmth, and then I felt the Holy Spirit touch me. For the first time in as long as I could remember, I felt a twinge of what I now realize was hope. This was something I had not felt in such a long time. It was Thursday night, church night for Solid Rock South. They asked me to get in the van and go to church with them. I knew I had to go. I walked into church in a white wife beater, black bandanna and my backpack. I was surprised when I walked in and the first person I saw was my friend Andrea from high school. She had recently returned to town from the Mercy Home in Tennessee and it had been awhile since we had seen one another. This was all seeming a little surreal as she looked at me and said "Don't you see what God's doing?" I met Miss Martha at this service, a pillar of the church. She told me to throw my cigarettes away, so I did. I threw them in the trash. James, one of the men that had been in the van, and the head of the Prison Ministry, put my phone number in his phone. As I walked out the door that night, I paused, picked my cigarettes back up out of the trash and went home. I was still carrying pride and had the attitude that I didn't need help from anyone. I could do this on my own. I didn't trust anybody, but yet I felt like something was now different.

For two weeks James would text me every day to check in and see how I was doing. At first I found it somewhat annoying. But gradually the realization set in "this man cares about me and he doesn't even know me. Why? Why would he care about me and what happens to me"? At this point in my life, everyone else had pretty much given up on me. That kind of unfailing love was a foreign concept to me having never been shown love in that way. I was from a world of drugs and illicit behavior and the only time anyone acted as though they cared, was when they wanted something from me.

I had taken a side job in West Virginia and would travel back and forth. One day I came home from work and saw my sister sitting on the porch crying. I sat down beside her and asked "Why are you crying?" She said "I've been praying." Praying? That was odd. I didn't know my sister to be one that prayed. She handed me a flyer and I still recall the blue lettering on the white tract that said "Are you sick and tired of being sick and tired?" My sister had been handed this earlier that day by a ministry whose purpose was to go into the streets and save drug addicts. They would take them in, rise them up to be new pastors, and then send them into the inner cities to bring hope to other drug addicts. My sister was at a point she had to choose between her husband and her brother and she was starting to feel broken as well. I loved my sister and didn't want to hurt her. I felt a tugging in my heart and knew I had to go. At this point I had tried everything else; 12 step programs, Narcotics Anonymous, court ordered programs and nothing helped. At this point I had nothing to lose so I decided I might as well give this Jesus guy a try. With my bags packed, I headed for United Restoration Ministries in the Over the Rhine district of Cincinnati.

They were expecting me when I arrived. They met me at the front of the building and advised that before I came in I had to throw away my cigarettes and say the sinners prayer, asking Jesus into my heart. As I walked into the building I saw 40 men praying in the sanctuary. Tattooed, pierced, scarred – these men were not like the young female counselor I had met at the recovery center during high school. These men were hardened criminals, yet they had such a sense of peace about them as they prayed out loud to the God who had saved them. I wanted that peace, I had longed for that rest in my soul for as long as I could remember.

This ministry is not a twelve step program; it is a one step program. You talk to the only one who can fix it, accept Him into your heart and your slate is wiped clean. You claim victory and stand on the promise in *2 Corinthians 5:17 "All that come to Christ are new creations. Behold old things are passed away, all things become new."* You will never hear these men say they are "recovering" – they are "set free", "delivered" and no longer who they used to be. You can't move forward if you carry around the chains and titles of your past. I found the other programs I had been involved in as depressing and lacking hope as they carried the "once an addict, always an addict" perception.

I had only been there a couple of days when I awoke from a dream where I was saying "Ephesians". What was Ephesians? Was that a book in the bible? I asked one of my counselors who told me it was indeed a book in the bible. I had been questioning if this was truly happening? Was I really saved and starting a new life? It all still seemed just a little too surreal. As I opened my bible to Ephesians Chapter 2 I read *"Once you were dead because of your disobedience and your many sins. You used to live in sin, just like the rest of the world, obeying the devil – the commander of the powers in the unseen world. He is the spirit at work in the hearts of those who refuse to obey God. All of us used to live that way, following the passionate desires and inclinations of our sinful nature. By our very nature we were subject to God's anger, just like everyone else. But God is so rich in mercy, and he loved us so much, that even though we were dead because of our sins he gave us life when he raised Christ from the dead. (It is only by God's grace that you have been saved!) For He raised us from the dead along with Christ and seated us with Him in the heavenly realms because we are united with Christ Jesus. So God can point to us in all future ages as examples of the incredible wealth of his grace and kindness towards us, as shown in all He has done for us who are united with Christ Jesus. God saved you by his grace when you believed. And you can't take credit for this; it is a gift from God. Salvation is not a reward for the good things we have done, so none of us can boast about it. For we are God's masterpiece. He has created us anew in Christ Jesus, so we can do the good things he planned for us long ago."* As I found and read that chapter it spoke to my heart. It was at this moment that God first become real to me and it weirded me out just a bit. I read it with a clear understanding and knew it was God speaking to my heart. I still get excited about that first rhema word God gave me. It spoke to my heart so strongly. This is one of the first moments that God had become real in my life and it actually freaked me out. I don't know how to explain what I felt that morning, but it was almost like a blindfold had been taken off my eyes and God allowed me to see Him for who He is. In the past I just believed, I didn't know what it meant to have a personal relationship with Jesus and this was the beginning of that. Even though it had scared me, I was intrigued by this and it made me hungry for more.

We would wake up at 5:30 am and pray for an hour before leaving at 9am and going to the inner city streets all around the country, wherever we felt lead to go. While there we would witness and hand out flyers. Once a week, we would do something called a "blasting" setting up speakers and playing music and giving our testimonies. As I read my bible and prayed on a daily basis, and went out to the streets, God started to become more and more real to me. God performing miracles started to become the norm as He put people in our path who were crying out for help. These meetings were not a coincidence, they were divine appointments by God. I started to see Him move in my life as well as the lives of those around me. God had brought me hope with those people in the parking lot and was now using me to bring that same light to those bound in darkness. It was such an overwhelming feeling to be used by God. The peace that passes all understanding had settled on my heart. I now had hope and a promise for a future, something I thought I would never be able to attain.

In the early days of my stay God gave me discernment while I was there; what people to stick around who would help me grow spiritually. Normally one stays at the ministry for 9 – 12 months. On the 9th month the Lord put it on my heart to stay longer. I became a counselor, started teaching bible studies and began to run a room. God was preparing me for my next step.

After being there for two years, I was given a pass for a week long family visit. I took that visit to not only see family but visit the church that had picked me up from the streets. My friend Andrea invited me to attend a service at Solid Rock South; The church where the van of street evangelists had found me in my broken state and said a prayer that started a ripple in my life. Pastor Jason was speaking that morning and the title of his sermon was "Begin Again". That sermon touched me and stirred something in me that had been a tugging in my spirit. Was it time to come home? Was it time to begin again where I came from and help others? As that stirring started to rise in my heart, I started praying and asking God to guide me.

I had been deep in prayer all week about receiving confirmation if I was to stay or go back home. The next Sunday morning, back at the ministry, before church I prayed and asked God for confirmation. The title of the sermon that day? "Confirmation". By the time the sermon was over, I knew it was time for me to go home. I packed my bags and headed back home that night.

When I got back home I didn't have a job, but I had learned the importance of being around like-minded people. While the location was the same, the environment was different this time. I had to change the people I hung out with, the music I listened to, the places I went. I went to the church every day from 9-5 to work for the church as a volunteer while I waited on a job. Idle hands and an idle mind is the devils playground, so I got plugged in on Monday nights at the church with their prayer services. Every time the doors were open, I was there. As I got plugged in, I began to meet like-minded people on the same mission I was on. You have to pursue God with the same intensity you used to pursue that next high.

I got hired to go back to the out-of-town job in West Virginia, but I didn't like being gone. I started praying for a job that would afford me the opportunity to attend and work in the church. Two weeks later I got a job at Home Depot. I wasn't there long until I started to get awards and a promotion. I witnessed to my co-workers and walked this walk with a holy boldness. It wasn't long until God brought me an even better job with more money and benefits. With that job I was able to buy my first vehicle. Life was finally becoming normal. Something I had waited on and longed for my whole life.

You can pray for yourself, but it's when you put your desires aside and start to pray for others, that's when God starts answering your prayers. My mom saw the change in me and she started attending church and got saved. You get blessed when you are a blessing to someone else. I got involved in the Prison Ministry, serve at Masters Kitchen and go with the Living Free class to the rehab facility in New Richmond. The Holy Spirt now filled the void that I once tried to fill with anything and everything my flesh desired. Do not believe the lies of this world and secular programs that tell you once you are a drug addict, you are always a drug addict. If you believe in Jesus Christ, then you must believe in the word. And if you believe in the word, you must believe he is a deliverer. You will never hear me use the word "recovering" it gives you an excuse to fall back. I also want readers to know it wasn't an instant transformation. *"Be not conformed of this world but be ye transformed by the renewing of your mind"*. The only way to renew your mind is to wash yourself in the word. Speak life into every situation, no matter how dark it seems. Surround yourself with people of light that will encourage you during your transformation. You are never too far gone that God can't pick you up and bring you out of any situation you are in.

Author's Note: As I interviewed Aaron for this book we were sitting outside on a warm summer's night at a local coffee shop. He said to me, "You see that burger joint over there? A year ago I ran into a guy I had robbed once and sold drugs to. But that night I led him to the Lord." I have no doubt about why God brought Aaron back home. Those who knew him when he was bound by chains of addiction, anger and abuse now see him with his chains broken and living free. Others who are bound by similar chains look at him now and find hope and want to know how that happened. Our walk carries more weight than our words.

As Aaron said to me "We can tell others about Jesus and his transforming power and love, but each individual has to get to a point that they seek him until he becomes real to them. That's when the transformation begins and the chains fall to the ground." He also said that while he's been clean for four years now, he feels it's important not to count the days like the ability to slip is just around the bend. Once you are healed, you are healed and a new creature. You are no longer an alcoholic or drug addict, you are a child of the King and you are free!

Aaron and I both pray that if you are reading this and struggling with abuse and addiction, you take the first step of starting your journey to your One Step Program by finding a relationship with the only true healer, Jesus Christ.

"Those who are wise will shine as bright as the sky, and those who lead many to righteousness will shine like the stars forever." -Daniel 12:3

CHAPTER 4
HOSTAGES OF HEROIN

Heroin is a very real problem that is sweeping every corner of the United States. This epidemic does not discriminate as it claims lives without regard to color, economic status or age.

"Hope Over Heroin" is a vision to create a "net church" by tearing down denominational walls and becoming the hands and feet of Jesus. On August 8th, 9th & 10th, 2014 at that first Hope Over Heroin event in Hamilton, OH that vision became a reality as 30 churches came together as one united body of believers, bringing hope to the hopeless. Many of those whose lives were transformed would not have felt comfortable coming into a church. God used his faithful to meet them where they were.

Looking back at the pictures of the sea of thousands of people at the Montgomery County Fairgrounds "Hope Over Heroin" I didn't see a group of lost souls or addicts. God spoke to my heart and said "This is the beginning of a great revival!" These are new souls full of hope and promise, and this is going to be BIG! Suddenly I saw how this epidemic that quietly swept our land touching the rich and the poor, every race, every denomination, how this will be used to once again make beauty for ashes like God has done so many times before. Free will allows us to make bad choices, but we also have the ability to find forgiveness and hope! To choose life! Many believe Heroin is the worst addiction, almost impossible to get free and the statistics show, many end up dead. I've spoken to a lot of recovered addicts who have told me "It was the fear of withdrawal that kept me hooked. I wanted to get clean, but the fear of withdrawal was greater than my desire to get clean." That fear causes addicts to lie, steal, overdose and eventually die.

But there is good news! I was there that summer and I watched hundreds at the end of the services get baptized and when they came up out of the water, they threw their needles on the ground and walked away! Many of those are still coming to church, months later, free from the addiction pursuing God with the same intensity they used to pursue that next high. I have met many former addicts who tell me proudly and without flinching that there is power in the name of Jesus! How they got supernaturally healed and suffered no withdrawals. Those people have become testimonies to other addicts, to their families and friends who have watched their lives become instantly and totally transformed. If someone can get delivered from Heroin, then there is hope and freedom from any addiction, any depression or fear.

"For I have not given you a spirit of fear and timidity, but of power, love and self-discipline." – 2 Timothy 1:7

Visit www.hopeoverheroin.com for more information & schedule

CHAPTER 5
SURVIVING LOSS

I woke up New Year's Day and settled onto the couch with my cup of coffee, picked up my phone and clicked on the Facebook icon. I saw a "Who knows a good DUI lawyer" post, and those of others sharing the stroke of midnight with their families and friends. And then I started seeing posts appear that were of great concern. They were tagged to Paige, a beautiful young woman from my hometown and were reading: "So sorry to hear about your loss, we are praying for you..." My first thoughts were that a grandparent or parent may have passed. And then the post came that left me in a state of shock and stupor.... an immediate pain and heaviness on my heart for this beautiful young family. "I'm so sorry for the loss of your son." Reading that was surreal, surely there was a mistake? Their beautiful 4 month old son Lincoln had stopped breathing in the night. This is the caring young woman who raised money for another family to be able to have a child of their own; the young woman who owns the local salon where you are always greeted with a smile and feeling of warmth from her genuine, beautiful spirit. This is the momma always posting pictures and stories about her babies that we so enjoy reading.

I felt so helpless, the only thing I could do was go to prayer... "God this family believes in you and knows you; reveal yourself to them in a mighty way as they are left to deal with this loss. Wrap them in your peace and love. This is the type of thing that makes non-believers doubt your existence. They can't see YOU are the only way to get through something like this. This is the type of thing that can shake even the believers. Please be with these parents and give them strength, peace and an abundance of faith."   I prayed for them off and on all day as I thought of the grief they must be experiencing, as I thought of how our lives can change in one instant and we will never be the same. From the Facebook posts I read, an entire community was praying and sending their love to this precious family.

As my heart was still grieving for the family the next day, I opened up my Facebook to read these posts from the mother and father of baby Lincoln. This couple had just experienced loss, and yet they were posting words of encouragement for our souls and giving us a lesson in unwavering faith.

"I just want to tell everyone thank you for your prayers and kind words. Lincoln James was an amazing sweet boy. I can rest easy knowing that my baby boy went to sleep last night and woke up to the face of our Lord. That's what I hold on too, that's all any of us can do kiss my girls goodnight and be in my husband's arms and dream of my son's new life with Jesus." - Paige

"But Jesus called the children to him and said, "Let the little children come to me, and do not hinder them, for the kingdom of God belongs to such as these." - Luke 16:18

"Thank you God for the son you sent Paige and me. Thank you God for the 4 wonderful months you gave us with my little buddy. Thank you God for the family and friends you have given us. Without God, family, and friends we could not go through this. I just know that our grandparents welcomed my son in heaven. I know they are tucking him in the way he loves, feeding my fat boy every 2 hours, and enjoying his contagious grin. We don't have our son to hold, but we have the memories. Knowing he is at peace, gives us some sort of peace on earth. We are hurting, but my God is working. Thank you so much to everyone for their thoughts, prayers, and kind words; We love each and every one of you so much!" – Codey

I read these posts and tears started to fall as I witnessed some of the most amazing testimonies of faith I have ever seen. It's easy to say we believe and have faith in the sunshine, but what about in the storms of life? That's when we have to grab ahold of our anchor, when our faith is tried, and it's when we become stronger. I read so many posts of how the parents were the ones comforting those that came to the services for their precious baby boy. I have witnessed this tragedy bring a community together in prayer and love. Their story has made many pause and stop to think about Jesus and where our hope comes from; for parents to appreciate their own children just a little bit more and hug them just a bit tighter. I have no doubt in my heart that this is a beginning in an end. These parents and their steadfast faith will rise above this tragedy and hold to God's promise to make beauty for ashes. Their story has already been a witness to hundreds and in the future they will become a comfort to those who will suffer a similar loss. While their beautiful baby boy was only here a short time, the impact of his life will surely be eternal.

I posted the story above on my blog, within three days 7,000 people from as many as nine countries had read the story of Little Lincoln. I contacted Paige to tell her that I truly believed while Lincoln's life here on this earth was short his story would have an impact far beyond what we would ever see. That lives would be saved and transformed by their story. That someone else suffering from the loss of a child may once again gain hope and peace from their example.

In time, Codey found a source of strength in his grief process by writing. Below is his testimony about the loss of a son, as taken from his blog....

Why?

In essence of grieving, I have found that writing can be an asset to healing. It has taken me two weeks to gain the courage to put my emotions on paper. This experience has obviously been the most difficult endeavor I have ever faced. This blog will cover my view of the tragic loss of my son Lincoln James Juillerat.

December 31st, 2014 at approximately 11:00am, I remember typing a post on my Facebook. As I was typing this post, I was holding my son. He was very vibrant and happy in that moment. I remember having trouble typing the post because Lincoln would not stop smiling at me. His smile was contagious. There were a couple agendas to complete on this day. The first was to take Paisley (our oldest daughter) to Cincinnati Children's Hospital for her tonsil consultation. Paige and I had a great time with Paisley. As parents of three, spending alone time with each child was a difficult task. I was my typical self, and told Paisley that alligators were going to eat her tonsils out. She is getting too smart for her own good, and she can now sniff my jokes out without a flinch. After the doctor's appointment, we took Paisley to my in-laws. They were watching all of our children that night, so that Paige and I could enjoy some time celebrating the New Year. Before we left my in-laws, I kissed each of my children good-bye. I rarely loved on Lincoln, but this night I did (thank God). He was so happy, as he kicked and cooed the entire time I loved on him. By 7:00pm, Paige and I were heading to my parent's house to enjoy an evening without our children. When we arrived at my parent's home, we began playing euchre while striking up conversation. Much of the night was erased from my memory until 12:06am, January 1st. We just got done watching the ball drop, and Paige's phone rang.

Paige listened and immediately said, "Mom your joking (ha ha) right?!?! This is a joke?!"

They both hung their phones up. Paige instantly called her mother back, and the news was confirmed that this was not a joke. My four moth old son stopped breathing while he was asleep in his bed. We did not know anything more at this point. We ran to our van, while my cousin drove us to the hospital. The drive consisted of screaming, yelling at God, hope, praying, cussing at God, and many more emotions. We arrived at the hospital in Greenfield, and had an EMT telling us that we could not enter a specific door. The EMT was unaware that the infant he just transported was my son. I ran up to the door, and pulled the locked door apart and entered the hospital with Paige. As we ran around the corner, any hope of my son living was dismantled. I could see the hurt and pain in my minister's eyes. I was told that through these tragic events, your body has a natural amnesia that helps you forget moments during the event. This is true, because I only remember four moments once inside the hospital while I looked at my lifeless son from a distance; I remember Paige yelling at the EMT's to stop administering CPR to Lincoln. I remember waking up on the floor, due to passing out once I saw Lincoln. I remember running outside, and yelling at God and screaming "Why" and "you are not real – you are not powerful." I remember my heart hurting. This hurt was not just a phrase, but a deep hurt that felt incurable. The thoughts rushed my head as we drove away from the hospital. This was not real! This is all a dream and I cannot wait to wake up so I can hug and squeeze my little boy. I couldn't wait to hear him cry for his bottle. Reality set in as I laid wide awake at 6:00am on January 1st, my son is dead. My sweet, innocent, loving son of four months is gone. All of my dreams and aspirations of a father and son connection were gone.

Days passed by, family and friends reached out for support, but my mind was gone. I went through the motions as each day passed, but my heart was with my boy. Anger would build up so heavy that I would have to walk outside and cuss at God. I kept thinking, what a joke. I have seriously wasted 27 years of my life believing in this God, and this is how I am treated?!

Sunday, January 4th, 2015 we buried my son's body. I was significantly struggling on this day. I played this emotionless man all day, until our family and friends said their final goodbyes. The hurt came flooding back as I hugged and held each one of them as they passed through the line. Once every one had passed, Paige and I were left alone with Lincoln to say our goodbyes. As we held onto each other, we sobbed and hurt together while shaking from the cold. This was so painful, and unbearable. I remember closing my eyes and praying to God. I prayed to a God who I hated, questioned, and cussed at a few days earlier, but now I asked him to make sure Lincoln was taken care of. In an instant my body became warm; the sounds of the wind and trees drowned out, and my tears were almost wiped away. I asked Paige if she "felt that." She confirmed she did, and simultaneously we walked away thankful for the comfort God gave us. I was not going to leave my son, but God's reassurance gave me the strength to walk away. The warmth and drowning sound was almost as if God said, "It's okay, I have Lincoln and you two do not need to worry." My faith instantly erupted to a level of no return. God is real and Lincoln is okay.

I sit here two weeks later typing this story, attempting to evaluate the roller coaster of emotions I have experienced. Let me first say that I am a sinner. I am not worthy of God's grace, I am not even worthy of the family he has blessed me with. Without being a biblical guru, I have attempted to read and understand God more. What better way to do that, than to open the Bible. I came up with a couple things:

1. Becoming a Christian is easy, remaining a Christian is hard. As Christians, we are afflicted with many trials. God doesn't cause these trials, but God is watching how we respond. In the Bible, in John 16:33 Jesus states, "I have told you these things, so that in me you may have peace. In this world you WILL have TROUBLE. But take heart! I have overcome the world."
Jesus clearly states that even Christians will struggle. We are human and we make millions of mistakes. But if we "take heart," we are reassured that our God is greater. Lincoln's death hurts me from the bottom of my soul. I selfishly want my son back, but my son didn't struggle. Like Paige has said, "He fell asleep, and woke up in the arms of Jesus." Amen!

2. "Where are you God? Why do I deserve this pain?" You cannot read the Bible, and understand suffering until you read the book of Job. Job was a faithful man who was extremely wealthy, and blessed with a wonderful family. As Job endures many trials, he holds onto his faith. At the end of Job's trials, God rewards Job for his faith by giving him double the life he had prior to his trials. We may never know "why," but God's plans are greater than Paige and I can ever fathom. In Isaiah 55:9 it states, "As the heavens are higher than the earth, so are my ways higher than your ways and my thoughts than your thoughts." Through Lincoln's death, as hard as it is to imagine, God has a plan greater than I can imagine. Paige and I have stated multiple times, that if Lincoln's passing means that one more person will get saved and follow Christ, then this was all worth it. We truly mean this, but it still doesn't take the sting away from losing Lincoln. We are still human, living on earth, striving for God's purpose. The main thing to realize through these tragedies is that God does not give them to us. Many people hold on to the cliché saying, "God only gives us what we can handle," I disagree. God does state that throughout our lives we will face trials and struggles, but he does not individually hand them out like a parent spanking their child. He promises us that he will be with us through it all. The saying should state, "God will be with us as we walk through the halls of hurt and pain."

3.Closing – Trying to function in this world with any kind of sanity is a difficult feat. I can't imagine how someone would get through this without faith. Knowing where I get my strength makes the days bearable. My all-time favorite verse in the Bible comes from Philippians 4:13, "I can do everything through him who gives me strength." I began reading a book by Jefferson Bethke titled, "Jesus > Religion," when Paige was in labor with Lincoln. I haven't picked the book back up until yesterday. As I was reading it I found an excerpt that stated, "You find a person who truly believes in God, and you'll find a person who can't be touched. He or she may be bruised, beat up, and hurt by this life, but nothing can reach his or her life because it isn't even here." I couldn't find a quote from the book more relevant to my life than this one.

Our lives will be presented with storms, but after the storm calms, the potential for spiritual growth conforms. We can either grow with our experiences, or we can sit miserably in self-pity asking WHY? My family will continue to love God, treat people fairly, and help those who need it. Lincoln's life will always hold a huge part in my heart. I will never forget the feeling of achievement and satisfaction, when I found out we were having a boy. I will never forget the hurt and anger from losing my boy.

Looking forward, I will never let myself forget through God's grace Paige and I had a beautiful son whose little heart wrapped an entire community together. Lincoln's life purpose is not finished. *Story by Codey Jullierat - Lincoln's daddy.*

Lincoln's Grandmother Penny posted the following on her Facebook wall a couple of weeks after the loss of Lincoln: *"When something bad happens you have three choices. You can let it define you, let it destroy you, or you can let it strengthen you."* This family's strength is truly a testimony of what faith in God can pull you through.

CHAPTER 6
CHAINS OF UN-FORGIVENESS

August, 2012: A few short months prior I moved an hour away from life as I had known it for 46 years. In one quickly chaotic weekend there was move to a new town, the start of a new job, and the beginning of a new chapter in my life. That move should have been our final "good bye", but instead, we chose to continue to see each other on the weekends as we put one another through that final few months of hell. While we had shared many special moments those last seven years, we had also hurt one another deeply during that time with mistakes, lies and deception. But as we stood on opposite sides of the kitchen counter that day, we were once again friends in that last moment. He took out a piece of paper and as he drew a picture for his analogy, he spoke to me as a friend who cared about my soul. As he drew, he spoke these words "You are like this big, beautiful blimp...something you don't see every day. You glide across the sky almost effortlessly, and people stop to watch you from afar. You fly along with what appears to be ease, but the truth is, you still have some chains hanging from you that most can't see." He illustrated by drawing chains hanging off the blimp as he continued: "There is a chain of un-forgiveness for things you have done. You must forgive yourself." "There is a chain of fear to trust others because of the hurt you have endured as well as inflicted." "There is a chain of insecurity and doubt." These chains can get tangled up in one another as you fly along. When they get tangled you are no longer flying along in a straight path, but instead flying in circles, going nowhere. You need to break those chains off so you can once again fly free with direction and purpose, reaching your destination. Tears filled my eyes as he spoke those words to me and they settled in my soul. He was right.

It was a warm summer evening when I walked into Solid Rock Church for the first time. From the moment I walked in, I knew that I was where I was supposed to be. Confirmation came at the end of the service when the worship leader started singing a song I had never heard before. The song was "Break Every Chain". Warm tears streamed down my face as I watched the words on the screen "There is power, in the name of Jesus, to break every chain…" . The people around me were raising their hands in the air to give praise to a God who had broken their chains and set them free. I could feel God's grace and love in my heart and soul and felt the chains that had kept me flying in circles being broken off. I forgave myself for the things I had done to hurt others and for those who had hurt me. Insecurity, doubt and fear had to go in the presence of my savior. I was left full of hope and love and a desire to get back on the path that was set before me. It was time to jump off the treadmill of bad choices and bad relationships and discover who I was in Christ.

I felt like a modern day woman at the well. Jesus spoke to my heart "I have been sitting here waiting on you for a long time. I have watched you. You believe in me, you know I hold the answers and you have faith. I have seen your heart full of love, yet you have let past hurts cause you to look for your worth in the acceptance and love of others. You have made mistakes that have hurt your soul and those around you. This has left you lonely and thirsting for more when those you loved have taken their love away. Let me show you the living water that will keep you from ever thirsting again. The water that will satisfy your soul, give you hope and set you free!" I am proud to say that by the grace of God, my cup is running over with living water!

This knowledge of who I am in Christ, fearfully and wonderfully made, has healed me and made me whole. It has allowed me to love myself again. And this blimp is back on course to reach her destination and purpose.

Step one on my journey and possibly yours, Realizing who you are in Christ: *"**Therefore if any man be in Christ, he is a new creature: old things are passed away; behold, all things are become new.**" 2 Corinthians 5:17.* Don't listen to those thoughts that you are a lost cause and that you have done so much wrong you can never be forgiven. Those are lies meant to keep you on the highway for destruction. The bible says that when you are forgiven, your slate is wiped clean and you can start anew. In the beginning it can be a battle for your soul. You may take 5 steps forward, only to find yourself going 3 steps backward or 5 steps backward. The important thing is to press in and keep moving forward. Keep seeking God and His will for your life. Eventually it gets easier as your relationship grows and you'll find yourself moving quite a few steps forward and rarely taking a few back.

I didn't hear the song "Break Every Chain" rededicate my life and suddenly everything was rainbows and Skittles. In fact, it was quite the opposite. I recall days of not wanting to wake up when the alarm went off because it meant the loneliness would soon follow and have a strong grip on me. I would go to work numb, the voices in my head saying "You have messed up so many times you will NEVER find love again. You don't deserve to love or be loved. You had your chance, and you blew it. You will be lonely and miserable for the rest of your life." Those thoughts would cripple me and put me in a dark place as I tried to function and pull off the façade of being happy and normal. It was the devils attempt at pushing me back, trying to keep me focused on the idea that I was worthless and unworthy if I didn't have a man who loved me. All the while there was someone who loved me, and He had never stopped, but I couldn't see that then. I still had a job to do, there were still people to interact with, I had to keep moving even though I felt like I was walking through the day with cement shoes on. That battle lasted almost two months, and then I heard the sermon that helped change things and push me to that next level of healing.

Pastor Lawrence preached a sermon in those first couple weeks I started attending this church and he spoke of a rhema word. I had grown up in church my entire life, but this was new to me. In his message he told how during his days of depression he was on his knees, crying out to God for a promise, for his rhema word for that time in his life and he shared with us the word that God gave him and what it meant to him. He told how he carried that promise with him and stood on it until he saw a breakthrough. I left the service and I wanted and need to know more. I came home and researched it (after I learned how to spell it). And this is what I read: In Greek, the word "rhema" means "an utterance". So in biblical terms, it means an "utterance from God". A rhema word is often given to a believer who is seeking God's will and guidance in the scriptures and it is usually timely, applying to a situation at hand. In 2 Timothy 3:16,17 the Apostle Paul writes: "All scripture is inspired by God and is used to teach us what is true and to make us realize what is wrong in our lives. It corrects us when we are wrong and teaches us to do what is right. God uses it to prepare and equip his people to do every good work." If we believe that the Holy Spirit guided the words of those who wrote the bible, we can believe that the while reading it, the Holy Spirit can speak to us through those same scriptures.

It was a beautiful, sunny Saturday. I had made the mistake of opening Facebook on my phone and it seemed as though every post was a family on vacation at the beach, a family out enjoying the sun on their boat or watching their child play soccer. It seemed as though everyone in the world was out living, loving and laughing, except me. The loneliness started to come back and I could feel the darkness trying to close in. I got down on my knees and I prayed "Please God, take this hurt and loneliness from me. Give me a promise to stand on during this difficult time. I want a rhema word!" And then I took my bible and closed my eyes and let the pages fall. I stopped and as I read in Hosea, I felt God speak to my heart. This was the rhema word He gave me: *"But I will court her again, and bring her into the wilderness, and speak to her tenderly there. There I will give back her vineyards to her, and transform her valley of troubles into a door of hope. She will respond to me there, signing with Joy as in days long ago in her youth.."* *Hosea 2: 14,15* I read that word and immediately I saw myself as a young girl attending that church in Centerfield and singing with my mother as she played the piano. How much faith and hope I had at that time when I was close to God and listening for His voice. I saw my vineyards as a home full of love and family and I had a vision of a house full once again. I felt God saying "You're in the wilderness now, but it's so you can grow and find Me once again. And when the time is right, I will not forsake you. I will restore what you've lost (a relationship) and transform your valley of troubles (tears, loneliness, regret) into a door of hope! I wrote that verse down in my journal, on post it notes and hung it on my refrigerator, my desk at work, in my car and whenever I would start to feel a bit down, I reminded myself of the promise and stood firmly on it. I didn't know how God was going to restore me, or how long it would take. I was still mistakenly thinking it meant I would have a relationship with a man and I wasn't even dating anyone. But I knew that God can make a way where there is no way, and boy did He ever!

Within only a couple of weeks of standing on that promise, things started to change. After I spent my time in the wilderness, He started to bring me out and back into the sunshine. My immediate family went from 3 to 8 in just a short time. My oldest son called and said "Mom, I want to ask Stephanie to marry me. Will you go with me when I shop for a ring?" My heart was overjoyed, the start of my vineyards being restored. And then the next surprise came. My youngest son told me he had been dating someone for a while, but they wanted to see where it went before they told anyone. Within another month I had 3 beautiful young girls and their mother in my life. Young girls who loved me unconditionally, who made me smile and laugh and warmed my heart as they wanted to spend time with me. I went to their ballgames, I took them to church and I loved on them whenever I could. My vineyards were being restored in ways I never even imagined and the loneliness was becoming but a distant memory. I often told the girls about my rhema word and reminded them that they are special and God used them to bless me and remind me what true love is all about. They would give me those sweet smiles as they pondered a God who cares for us and who hears our prayers.

I had that verse in my car until it got weathered and faded. Until the promise came to pass and loneliness no longer filled my days and depression was but a distant memory. I was cleaning out my car recently and found that piece of paper in the door. It seemed as though those days were so long ago, when in fact it was only a little over a year ago. Wow! What an awesome transformation that had taken place in my life. Once you start to have faith and believe, fasten your seat belts and hold on – it's going to be an amazing ride!

"Because of Christ and our faith in Him, we can now come boldly and confidently into God's presence." – Ephesians 3:12

The second step in my healing was to believe the promises available to me. In John 4:13, 14 while talking to the woman at the well, Jesus replied, "Anyone who drinks this water will soon become thirsty again. But those who drink the water I give will never be thirsty again. It becomes a fresh, bubbling spring within them, giving them eternal life." I once dreaded waking up and facing the day. I now wake up eager to see what adventures the day will hold and what amazing things I am going to see.

December 31, 2014: New Year's Eve, I sat here in reflection realizing I could never have fathomed just how great of a year was in store for me! I sometimes feel I lived more life in 2014 than I did in the 47 years prior. The "2014 Year In Review" movie trailer plays in my head with snippets of "True Love Week", "Hope Over Heroin", street witnessing with Cheeseburgers and Jesus. I had a son who got married and I gained a beautiful daughter in law, while another son moved away to start a new career and made me so very proud of his fearlessness to pursue his dream. Being sworn in as a Guardian ad Litem and CASA Volunteer and then taking on my first case and becoming the voice of a child. Listening to God's nudging to help start His clothes ministry at the church, performed random acts of kindness and experienced many amazing Jabez moments all because I listened to that still small voice when it spoke to me and said to move. I created a web-site in memory of my mother and started the process of writing my first book, all while working a full time job. There were days it seemed my feet never touched the ground. I feel most blessed when I think of all the amazing, beautiful, strong, inspiring women I now call friends. Women I didn't know a year ago, and so many new friends that I can't find the time I wish I had to spend with all of them! My cup runs over with blessings and true agape love!

I look back on this past year in total awe when I think of where I was only a short 6 months prior to 2013. Sitting in depression feeling lost and confused; focusing on what I didn't have and the many mistakes I had made. I was 46 years old and didn't have a house paid for like many my age, a place my boys could come to and call "home". Instead, I was starting over in a small two bedroom apartment an hour away from family and friends. I scrolled through Facebook and felt even sorrier for myself when it seemed as though everyone was out with family or friends on the lake, at the beach on vacation, or at their children's sporting events while I sat home, alone. So what changed?

Why am I able to stand back and look at 2014 in total awe and amazement feeling blessed beyond measure??

Here is my secret: I turned off the TV, I turned off Facebook and stopped being envious of everyone else's lives and started living, with purpose, my own. I stopped making it about me, and stopped comparing myself to others. Instead of dwelling on what I didn't have, I thanked God every day for all the many blessings I did have. I not only spoke it, but I started seeing myself as blessed and asked Him to use me to help someone else; being more concerned with showing love to those around me who were hurting or struggling than being concerned with my situation. The best way to have friends? Is to be one. The best way to be blessed? Be a blessing to someone else.

I stopped waiting for the sign to fall out of the sky to tell me "This is what I want you to do" and instead, started walking in faith and pursuing God's will for my life; finding total freedom in surrender. Taking my hands off the wheel was extra tough for me as admittedly, I like to drive. I wanted God's will, but I wanted to tell Him how I thought He should fix things for me. Oh I bet He got a kick out of that! If you sit in your misery and say "Why me?" you will stay in your misery. If you stay in a state of anxiety and confusion trying to "figure it all out" on your own, you will stay in anxiety and confusion. When you give it up and say "I trust you God – You got this"! And then take that first step on your journey in faith, you begin to make progress. One step at a time, one day at a time. As you walk forward boldly and pursue God, doors will open for you to walk through. And in the same manner, doors will close. And later, sometimes much later, you are as thankful for the closed doors that kept you from harm as you are the open doors that brought you blessing. And then what happens? You look up and realize a year has passed and you have experienced amazing moments and are in awe of how one led right into another just by walking in faith. I wrote this verse down and hung it with Post-It notes in many places until I got it deep in my soul: "Joy comes as a by-product of confidence in God, not certainty, in ones circumstances."

"You intended to harm me, but God intended it all for good. He brought me to this position so I could save the lives of many people." – Genesis 50:20

CHAPTER 7
SICKNESS CAN'T STAY ANY LONGER

"Mommy my stomach really hurts!" Jody's mother felt the abdomen of her little four year old girl and was surprised at how hard it felt and distended it looked. She had been in discomfort for a few days now and wasn't getting any better. Her mother decided it was time to drive to the doctor's office. It was 1972 in rural Highland County, Ohio. Technology was limited but the doctor knew what they were dealing with as he examined little Jody. The mother sat in a state of shock and stupor as the doctor walked back into the room and advised Jody needed to be at the doctor at 7:00 a.m. the next morning, and that there was only one choice she needed to make at this point; Did she want to take her daughter to Columbus or Cincinnati? Both were an hour away, one to the north and one to the south, but Jody needed to get to a larger hospital with more technology and there was no time to waste. At four years old Jody was officially diagnosed with cancer in her right kidney. The doctors called it a Wilm's tumor. There was an operation to remove the tumor and little Jody started to heal. But they were not out of the woods. At five years old they found another tumor in her right lung. Once again Jody went for surgery to have part of her right lung removed. The surgery was followed up by radiation treatments which ravaged the body of the small child.

Jody's parents had always been people of faith. Jody's grandfather and great-grandfather were both ministers so her parents both knew that Jesus could heal. But like any parent, our natural reaction is to try to find the best doctors, the best medicine; we try to fix it ourselves. When that second diagnosis came, the realization hit her parents like a ton of bricks, they were helpless to help their daughter. The only one who could save their little girl was the one who gave her to them in the first place. They spoke to the chaplain in the hospital about faith and healing. Then Margy called every tele-evangelist she had heard of, her home pastor, and prayer warriors in her church, asking they begin a prayer chain. They both felt helpless, and that point they put everything in God's hands, including Jody. And that's when the freedom came, in that surrender; surrendering their daughter and the circumstances surrounding her to the Lord. Starting to execute their faith that He would heal her, and asking that His will be done.

Jody's parents prayed diligently. Her mother found the number to the Oral Roberts hotline. She called and asked for prayers for Jody. She called all of her friends and asked them to pray. She loaded Jody up and drove her to a small country church that was holding a healing service. Jody recalls lying in the pew being so very tired, she just wanted to sleep. And then she heard the preacher say her name. He was calling her to the front of the church. Little Jody stood there at the altar as the pastor touched her with the anointing oil and started to pray over her, along with the other members of the church. Jody felt Jesus reach down and touch her and felt the warmth of the Healer's touch running through her body. She told her mother when they were done praying "Jesus touched me!" And indeed he did! He touched her and healed her little body. Jody grew up like any other child and experienced life the same as they did. Her story was an inspiration and testimony of faith to her entire family. Later in life Jody married a good man named Earl, had two beautiful children of her own, raised and showed horses and all was going well.

Jody had been left with a heart murmur and had to have annual check-ups. Every year she went and every year the results were always good. But in 2012 she was hit with some results she had not been expecting. Jody went in for her normal, routine visit and was told that she was going to need heart surgery. A valve had started to calcify as a result of the radiation she had received as a child. She now faced choosing a surgeon. Jody went to God in prayer as she faced this decision. She went to an appointment with a potential surgeon and received confirmation when he said to her "I will do all I can for you with the talents I've been given. The rest will be up to you and God." She felt a peace that this was the man God was putting in her path.

The surgeon advised that she would only be in the hospital four or five days after her heart surgery. Complications arose after the surgery and Jody was not in the hospital five days, but 15. They were having a hard time taking her off of the ventilator that was allowing her to breathe. Twice they had to use the paddles on her to restart her heart. She could see her husband Earl watching with such a sadness and fear in his eyes and she wanted them to make him leave. If she were going to die, she didn't want him to stand by and watch it happen. She was crying out in her head but with the tube in her throat, she could not speak. She felt so helpless…. And then she drifted off to this vision. She had recently lost a dog named Baylee that she had for many years. She loved that dog so much and missed her terribly. In this vision she was walking on a beach and could see this fog and light and she wanted to go into the fog, but every time she tried to walk toward the water, her dog Baylee would get in-between her and the fog. It was as if she spoke to her heart and said "Now is not the time for you to go. You need to go back." She remembers hearing the surgeon bend down and speak to her saying "If you live or die it's no longer up to me. I've done all I can. It's now up to God." She surrendered to God, to His will and she gradually started to improve. The surgeon told her she was a miracle. That God's hand had definitely been in her still being here. She gradually got nursed back to health and was back on the go working, tending to her horses, being a wife and mother.

It had been almost two years since the heart valve replacement when Jody got news that an aunt had died, they were going on vacation and she was in the midst of a hectic time when she found a small lump on her chest. She didn't think anything of it and continued about her busy schedule. After her aunt's funeral, she saw a friend who was also a doctor and told her of the lump she had found. She encouraged her to not wait and to come into her office to be looked at. The doctor felt they should take a biopsy. Assuming it was just precautionary from her history, Jody wasn't too concerned. After the biopsy surgery she sat with her family awaiting the results. But once again it came, she felt herself sitting in a fog trying to comprehend the words the doctor spoke "Your results show that you have breast cancer." Breast cancer?!? How can that be? I was healed as a child from cancer. There must be some mistake?!? But there was no mistake. She had breast cancer and they wanted to treat it aggressively. One of Jody's first thoughts was of her family... "Dear God please don't let this shake their faith!!" Her brother got angry and said "God healed you of cancer, this can't be cancer!" And she watched his faith start to waiver. The days following she endured a double mastectomy and all the side effects of the medication that went along with it. She lost her hair from the chemotherapy and radiation. She lost her fingernails and had sores in her mouth from the Tomaxifin she took. While the cancer ravaged Jody's body, it did not take her spirit or her faith. Jody knows that she has survived deaths door multiple times because God is not finished with her yet. She knows He has spared her to be a witness and an example. That she's here to teach her children and grandchildren about Jesus; to be an example that there is freedom in surrender to His will and He will be Jehovah Rapha, our healer. He will be the Prince of Peace and bring a calming to your heart, even in the midst of a mighty storm; a strong tower and source of strength to face every battle.

Jody's heart leapt for joy when she heard her brother had said he knew she was actually blessed to have this trial. It was her testimony that would give others hope and let them know Jesus is our healer. Her brother had prayed for a long time for peace and understanding with the struggles she had been having. And like he always does when we seek, God spoke to his heart giving him the realization that He is sometimes closest to us in the midst of our struggles. God uses our test to become our testimony; to encourage others fighting the same battle.

"For by me thy days shall be multiplied, and the years of they life shall be increased." – Proverbs 9:11

CHAPTER 8
A HEART ATTACK AND HEAVEN

I have always had a measure of faith. The necklace my grandmother gave me with a mustard seed floating in a pendant is still in my jewelry box. I recall that moment as a 5 year old little girl, digging through her jewelry box and stumbling upon this treasure. She watched with a warm smile as I held up the pendant, contemplating the purpose of the mustard seed. That's when she said, "The bible says you only have to have faith the size of this mustard seed and you can do great things!"

I believe with the heart of a child in angels and the power of prayer. My mother died of pancreatic cancer in 2002 at the early age of 54, yet I did not lose my faith. My mother was instrumental in helping me find that type of faith through her example over the years. And while I miss her terribly, and don't understand why she had to go on to heaven at such a young age, I trust in God. I believe He has a plan for us all. I witnessed God be with my mother. Pancreatic cancer has been said to be one of the most painful types of cancer; yet I saw her in no pain in those moments the nurses and doctors would say, "but that doesn't make sense? With your vitals and condition you should be in pain." I saw a peace in her eyes as God sent His love and grace to sustain her, as well as us, through a difficult time. My logical human brain tried to make sense of her dying just to help me deal with my own grief during that time. I saw family members start attending church or contemplating God through her witness and life testimony. In essence, her earthly death may have given her loved ones eternal life, which she already had awaiting her.

In August of 2002 my mother-in-law died of pancreatic cancer, in October of 2002 my mother died of the same illness. Shortly after my mother's death my grandma had to be admitted to a nursing home, where she later died. A young 17 year old boy from our small town who was a friend of my son's, died in a boating accident that spring. My sister-in-law suffered an aneurism and passed away that summer. My father-in-law died in November of 2003 and my grandfather passed in January of 2004. Death and sickness had surrounded me, yet I kept my faith in God realizing that while we may question His plan, sometimes there are things we do not know. I saw a billboard once outside a church that read "God gives you the test first, then you learn the lesson." I kept waiting for the test to be over and the lesson to be learned. At times I felt like Job, like I was being tested to see if I really did have a child like faith, or if I could be shaken. But then I resorted to God's promise, "I will not put on you more than you can bear." God must have been thinking I was one tough cookie!

At that time in my life I was starting every day off with a prayer to God asking him for traveling mercy for my children and family. I asked him to watch over and protect my family and to put us where we needed to be. I envisioned angels standing around my children's cars, their school, and I gave it all to God so I could get through my day without worry of things that were outside my control.

February 19th, 2004, I was returning from lunch and met my father at the traffic light. He was on his way to work for the day where he worked as a second shift Supervisor. I worked at the same company on first shift. He waved and my spirit stirred uneasy to the point I took notice. For some reason I looked at the clock in my car, and the time 1:08 pm stuck in my mind. I was at my desk, which was across the airport from my dad's office, when I got the call at 1:35 that he had collapsed in the parking lot and I needed to get to the hospital where he was being taken by ambulance. "Kris, he just went down.." the shaken voice on the other end of the phone was saying. What?!? My dad?!? Yet I knew what was happening. I had subconsciously feared this call my whole life. Dad was having a heart attack. For a while after my mom died I would get scared when I realized my dad was all I had left. I was only 35 when my mom died and I needed and wanted my parents. My boys needed grandparents. Gradually the fear of something happening went away, because hadn't God promised me He wouldn't put on me more than I could bear? I mean, I could not bear losing my father, not for many, many years. Dad had just been at the doctor on Monday and the doctor had told him not to worry about his heart, it was fine. What a false sense of security! But here it was, my worst nightmare, happening in real time.

I sat at my desk numb as I started shaking uncontrollably and saying "I can't do this again, I just can't." A dear friend who sat two seats away drove me to the hospital while another friend located my husband to meet us there. On the way to the hospital I tried calling my brother Wyatt. He wasn't home and I didn't have his cell phone number. I called the school where my sister-in- law Stacey was a teacher and luckily she was just walking by the office door when I called. I explained what was going on and she said she'd leave and find my brother. Trying to get ahold of those who needed to know, trying to comprehend myself what was happening, it was all an overwhelming blur.

Walking into the emergency room my heart sank. Everyone gave me "the look". I asked for dad and they told me I had to wait and speak with a nurse or doctor as they all lowered their eyes from mine and just looked at one another. I said, *"You don't understand, I know my father may be dying and I will NOT sit out here. I want to see him NOW!! You can either take me to him or I will find him myself!"* The doctor came through the door as I finished that bold, demanding statement. He told me that dad was unresponsive and not breathing on his own. He was still having a heart attack and they were doing all they could for him, but it didn't look good. They had called the Life Flight and if they could get him stable, they would fly him to Dayton.

They let me back there with him and told me to keep talking to him. He was white and cold, and was not there. I kept telling him I loved him and he couldn't leave me, not now. I told him that he was the strongest man I knew. They asked me to step out for a minute. It was such a blur, like a bad dream and surely I'd wake up soon... They handed me his money clip, his billfold and told me to make sure I got the bag with his clothes and shoes in it. A few minutes later a nurse found me and handed me his sunglasses. That's when I lost it! My dad always had his sunglasses. I started to cry and rebuke this; No, no, no! This can't and won't happen!

Nurses had led me back out to the desk so I could make some calls, they were helping by calling for me. A nurse called upstairs and wanted a social worker to come down and be there for me, just in case. They heard me saying I couldn't go through this again and knew my mom had died just a year and a half earlier. The lady on the phone behind the desk asked me "Is your dad from Leesburg?" I said "Yes", and then she said "Is your name Kris?" I said "Yes. Why?!?" She said, "Someone upstairs knows you and I need to call them." The desk had called the wrong number when they called for someone to help me, but in fact it turned out to be the exact right number. It was Susan and I needed her in that moment. She came down there holding me up and helping me. I told her I was so numb that I couldn't think straight. That I wanted to pray, but I didn't even know how to find the words. She and I went and sat down and she prayed for me when I couldn't. All I could do was say, "Jesus, Please!" I was also voicing my anger at the doctor my dad had just been to on Monday. While there, my dad told him he thought he was having heart problems. The doctor told him not to worry about his heart. That it wasn't his heart causing his arm and back pain. I was angry and looking to place blame in that moment. I was praying my brother would make it there before they flew dad to Dayton, just in case he didn't make it. Wyatt came right before they took off with him and he broke down like I did. It was just so surreal to see him lying there. Surely this was a bad dream and I'd wake up soon?

Susan went with dad out to the helicopter and prayed over him the whole way there. I prayed on the drive to Dayton that dad would be with good doctors and nurses when he got there, that they would make the right decisions. When we arrived at Dayton Heart, those people were looking at us with that same "look"...one of compassion and empathy for what we were about to have to face. I gave them the insurance information and a Physicians Assistant came out to talk to us. She told us that they thought Dad had been down quite awhile and they were unsure of his neurological state. Wait, I could help with that piece of the puzzle. Something had made me look down at the clock in the car and remember the time. I last saw him at 1:08. They said he was having a heart attack and they wanted to do a heart cath to go in and fix his heart. I was concentrating on getting the heart fixed and all the neurological talk was not concerning me; later it became clear that was their biggest concern. The longer he had been without air, the more chance for brain damage. I signed the consent papers for them to do the heart cath, we went to see him before they took him in, and then we went downstairs to wait.

With a waiting room full of family and friends for support, we sat and waited anxiously, as time seemed to stand still. Wyatt and I were then called into a room where the nurse told us all was going well. She then explained that those who found dad had used a piece of machinery called an AED that aided in saving his life. This machine reads your vital signs and takes the guess work out of determining if you need shocked or not. It was used on dad and shocked his heart back into a normal rhythm. She said the doctor would be out in a few minutes to talk to us. That was the longest 25 minutes, waiting to hear the fate of our father.

When the doctor finally arrived he explained the procedures his team had performed in an effort to save our father's life. We would soon be able to go to his room in intensive care.

We found him on life support and heavily sedated as we entered the room. We were all standing around and talking, feeling thankful and taking our first sigh of relief. We decided to take his rings off in case his fingers swelled up. Once we got them off, we heard the beep and watched the line on the monitor go flat...he was coding! What?!? Before I could even yell, 4 nurses busted in through the door. One jumped the 5 feet from the door to his bed and brought her fist down, hard, on his chest. That jolt got his heart beating again. The tape on the machine said he had been down only 9 seconds. That was like watching a scene out of a movie and it shook me to the core. It was one I wouldn't easily forget anytime soon. The doctor arrived and said that there had been minimal damage to his heart during the heart attack. He said that he would have to be on the life support system overnight and they would try to take it off the next day. It was still a question in their minds how long dad had been without air. Now that his heart was fixed, I was starting to realize their concern for neurological damage, similar to what a patient suffers with a stroke.

Dad's girlfriend Tammy wanted to spend the night at the hospital, so the rest of us went home. We got his truck from work and took it home for him. He had recently bought a new house and hadn't moved in yet. Wyatt went home and he and his best friend planted trees at the new place until 1:00 am. We believed that he was coming home. Doing those things to prepare for it kept us from feeling totally helpless. When we arrived home my son Matt said someone had called and said there were some heroes that had given dad CPR, but they didn't know who. I was anxious to learn more of that story and gather the missing pieces of the puzzle I didn't have. I don't think I got to bed until 1am and then I couldn't sleep. My mind kept racing wondering how long he had laid in the parking lot before someone found him? Who found him? What was on his mind when it happened? How much of that would he remember? At one time in that first Emergency Room I had the eerie feeling that it was probably playing out like a movie and he was watching me lean over him from above….maybe he did? Maybe he saw me begging him to come back. That night I kept having these dreams about dad, but they were good dreams. I woke with a peace about me, that peace that passes all understanding. I had the alarm set for 5 but didn't get up until 5:30. We headed back to Dayton.

Around noon on Friday a young man walked through the door of the hospital. His name was Tim. Tim had all the answers that I needed to the questions that had haunted me the night before. Tim said that for "some reason" he went to work early that day. He never went early, but that day he decided to and to then sit in his vehicle and study. He watched dad pull in the parking lot and get out of his big red truck. The truck was what caught his attention because dad usually drove his Mustang. But not that day. For some reason, that day, things were out of the norm. The truck caught Tim's attention and he watched dad get out, and then fall backwards, hitting the ground before he even got his truck door shut. Tim ran over and found he had no pulse and was not breathing. He started CPR and got him breathing, then went and got help. He found his girlfriend, Carol, who also worked there. She just happened to be going to nursing school. She came out and helped him work on dad until the EMT's got there. I can't even begin to explain the gratitude I felt towards him as I spoke with him. I told him I knew why he was there early, God had put him there. He seemed like such a sweet, tender hearted young man. He was visibly shaken and said he just had to come see dad and make sure he had not hurt him worse. I assured him that he had saved his life. The knowledge that dad hadn't lain there alone, and hadn't gone a long time without air, reassured me that it would be ok when they took him off life support.

I was getting off the elevator at the ground floor on Friday morning and there she stood, my person, my best friend Becky. I was so shocked and so happy to see her. She didn't have to say a word, she just hugged me. She hung in there with me all day. Her support meant so much. Many times she was left in the waiting room with my family. I didn't get to be with her the whole time, yet she was there for me. But then she always had been. God knew what he was doing when He brought us together as friends; and like He often does, He sent His love through her. I learned that day to never underestimate how much just being there for someone can be a blessing.

They decided to try and wean dad off the life support system around 3:00pm that day. Whenever they backed off the sedation medicine, he would come up fighting. They had his hands and feet tied to the bed. It was so hard for me to see him like this. I knew in my heart that even though he was heavily sedated, he was in there. I just prayed he didn't remember any of this! It was so hard for all of us to watch. The respiratory therapist said he thought he would come out of it ok. He kept saying how strong dad was when he saw him in the ER. That he had to sit on him and help hold him down. He joked he didn't want to meet him in a dark alley when this was all over with. Everyone was so nice and sympathetic to us. I didn't know at the time, and didn't find out until much later, that they all really had their doubts about what would happen when it was time to take him off the life support.

In the process, he had to breathe on his own with the machine off, but the tube in, for 15 minutes before they would take the tube out. That was the LONGEST 15 minutes! He was NOT happy! When they got the tube out he relaxed, then it wasn't long until he had his eyes open and knew us! AMEN!! Within the hour he was talking and laughing at some of the jokes we made. He kept asking over and over what happened? Stacey and I both noticed that when we told him what happened, when we got to the part about Tim and Carol giving him CPR, his expression would change. He looked and seemed so very sad, like he was remembering something. His chest was so sore from all the pounding. We kept reassuring him that it was fixed. It was odd because he knew who everyone was, and various other things, but every time he fell asleep and woke back up, we started over again like a groundhog day. He looked so scared and sad. I spent the night that night. I ended up pulling the recliner next to the bed so as he woke up throughout the night to ask me where he was and why he was there, I could just roll over and tell him. I didn't get much sleep that night, but I was so glad just to have him with us asking the same question over and over. I assumed it was just the coming out from under the medicine. By morning he was saying "So I had a heart attack?"

One day as I took a walk in the hallway of the hospital to clear my mind, one of the nurses came up to me and started to walk with me. She said "Honey, you do realize your dad is a miracle, right? We are all talking about the miracle that happened here." I just looked at her and before I could ask what she meant, she went on to say "When they brought him in he was foaming at the mouth and seizing. We've never seen anyone arrive in that shape and survive; and if so, not without brain damage. I was in the room with the doctors when one said "Just let him go. If we do save him he will be brain dead and the family will have to deal with that." But the other doctor, who was an answer to those prayers going up on my drive there that day said "But I have to try. These kids just lost their mother. I don't want to leave them without a father too." It was all starting to dawn on me just how much God's hand had been in this. From my knowing I needed to remember the time on the clock to Tim just happening to be at work early that day to my dad driving his big red truck that day that caused Tim to notice him, instead of driving the Mustang like he normally did. And then the receptionist at the hospital dialing the "wrong" number which turned out to be the number of a prayer warrior and friend; it was becoming more evident that there had been divine intervention.

We left the hospital with bottles full of medicine and unsure if he would fully regain his short term memory. At the point we left, he still had to write things down that he had done that day because he would forget. But I am blessed to be able to say that through continued prayers it wasn't long until his memory was fully restored! We witnessed the miracle of healing.

My dad is a no nonsense, no bull type of man; strong, silent, respected. He is a walking miracle. His being alive today is a result of "God moments". People being where they weren't supposed to be, doing things they don't normally do, all lined up to help save his life. He waited probably three or four months until he recovered to share this story with me. We were sitting in a doctor's office when he said to me "Did I tell you I saw your mom when I died?" No – wait – WHAT?!? He went on to say, "While I was dead (he was clinically dead for a bit) all of a sudden I was in this place where everything was beautiful. Colors that you can't even imagine, that we don't see here. I saw a woman coming to me in white over a bridge and it was your mom. I remember thinking "That's my Eleanor Mae...wait...she's dead...I must be dead too?" He said she took him by the hand and they sat on a bench and she was beautiful, glowing and her skin was radiant. She said to him "Now's not your time. The kids are crying out, they need you. You have to go back." He said the next thing he heard was my voice and the doctors and nurses saying "Come back to us"!! That story touched a couple of people in my family who knew my mom and knew my dad wasn't one to say much or make anything like that up. A couple of years later, I read that book "Heaven is for Real" and the little boy described "Bright, vivid colors we don't have here." that gave me such warmth and confirmation in my heart of what I already knew. There is a heaven and I will see my mother there again someday.

My mom died at a young age, my dad was spared. I never stopped believing or blaming God for any of it. In my mom's death, I became stronger and am able to carry on her legacy of helping others. My dad was spared and it helped him tell a story I can share to offer others hope. Some are spared, some are not. I am a walking testimony of many ways I've seen God's hand in my life. Answering prayers, but also shutting doors. And my having to learn that sometimes shut doors can actually be a blessing in disguise. I've had chains of guilt and un-forgiveness broken and been set free. I have survived depression and loss. I lost a 3rd pregnancy after my first two, but I've been blessed that I never lost my faith; even when things didn't make sense or hurt deeply. God is, and always has been, the lover of my soul. The only one who can bring that peace that passes all understanding.

"A man with an experience is never at the mercy of a man With an argument." - Anonymous

Kristina Thomas

CHAPTER 9
THE SECRET SIN

Pornography is an addiction just like any other drug. However, it's an addiction not often talked about that can wreck marriages and alter lives. For some, pornography is as addictive as crack cocaine. One exposure at the age of 13, at just the right time, and a child will grab that and it will become very much a part of them and be there for the rest of their lives. Studies show pornography is like any other drug. You take a little bit and it goes a long way, but then one gets bored with that and takes a little more and a little more. Soft core pornography such as Playboy, Penthouse, etc. is not illegal and how the addiction often starts for most. Research shows that teenagers are the number one buyers of both soft and hardcore pornography. Describing porn's effect to a U.S. Senate committee, Dr. Jeffrey Satinover of Princeton University said, *"It is as though we have devised a form of heroin ... usable in the privacy of one's own home and injected directly to the brain through the eyes."*

When any addiction; Drugs, Alcohol, Pornography is carried to its conclusion, the ultimate stage is death. In the bible in Romans 6:23 it clearly warns "The wages of sin is death." Many porn users find themselves getting aroused by things that used to disgust them or that go against what they know is morally right. This type of perverted porn is now over an 8 Billion dollar per year industry. Once they start watching extreme and dangerous sex acts, these porn users start to feel that those behaviors are more normal and common than they actually are; the desensitization begins. Sadly in the United States, the desensitization of our youth is happening at an alarmingly early age. Children are left to watch TV with no filter or monitor. Parents hand their children smart phones and tablets to "keep them quiet" while with one click of a button they can instantly see a porn video. Even if your child does not have a device, other children on the bus and at school do. I was speaking to a little eight year old girl recently who told me how the boys on the bus showed her a video of naked people; innocence lost at eight years old.

The porn industry is also linked to sexual trafficking and child abduction statistics that continue to climb alongside the sales of hard core, deviant pornography. Many will tell you that watching porn is harmless; but it is not harmless, on so many levels.

On a recent mission trip I attended a church service in Sturgis, South Dakota during the annual bike week event. A guest speaker at the church I was attending that Sunday stepped up front to share with the congregation why he was there. This man and his team were in town attempting to find and rescue women and children who were missing and had been abducted for sex trafficking. He told how their group had safe houses and partnered with professionals who would perform dental work and tattoo removal on these young victims once they were found and rescued. (Pimps often brand their abductees). There was a member of that church we were visiting who had an eight year old grandson who was stolen earlier that week. My heart ached for the mother and grandmother of that missing boy. The missionaries eyes filled with tears as he told us how he was driving down the road one day and a van pulled out in front of him and stopped. He could see a cute little girl in pigtails, likely eight or nine years old, sitting in the passenger seat. The man driving the van offered her up for sale, for whatever he would like to do to her. My heart broke in two, tears fell and I had a wave of nausea hit me as I heard this story. So many innocent lives are being lost to this horrific evil that is taking place in our world.

There is a website that I stumbled upon while doing research for this chapter. I found a lot of facts, statistics and stories on the site entitled "Fight the New Drug". It can be found on the web at www.fightthenewdrug.org . I encourage you to visit this website and get educated about the harmful effects of porn. There have been extensive studies completed and this website provides the results. It explains the ramifications of this addiction. Porn harms in 3 ways: It affects the brain, affects relationships and affects our society. Educate yourself and talk to your teen children. The best way to help prevent human trafficking is to be one more person refusing to watch porn.

I spoke with a young mother who chose to stay anonymous. I feel her story is worth sharing in this chapter. She told me how she had been a very devout Christian who loved the Lord and detested sin. She was a stay at home mom who felt she was in a good place in her walk. As a treat to herself, when the kids were laid down for a nap she had started watching a soap opera. The soap opera she watched day after day glorified affairs with exciting men and women. (*Her desensitization of what was acceptable and an altered reality began*). Over time she found herself feeling as though her life at home was boring and dull. She had read an article on-line describing how to spice things up in the bedroom. The article suggested watching pornography to get aroused or to provide new ideas. Although she knew it was wrong, she made the fatal click and started to watch. At first it seemed to spice things up, but then the problems started to arise. When watching the porn she felt like something took over her mind and body. She found it hard to explain to me, but said it was like she had this "different personality", one where she started to see sex as just a physical act between two bodies and was void of any emotion. Thoughts of her with random strangers started to creep into her mind. Instead of immediately dismissing those thoughts, she allowed herself to dwell on them. She ignored the warnings she had once read. The bible clearly states In 2 Corinthians 10:5 *"Casting down imaginations, and every high thing that exalteth itself against the knowledge of God, and bringing into captivity every thought to the obedience of Christ;"* But instead of casting down those evil thoughts and bringing them into captivity, she entertained them. She entertained them until she desired them. Until the porn no longer fed her newfound addiction. She loved her husband and her children, but she wanted and needed to experience the thrill she was now craving. This addiction caused her to eventually have an affair. One night when her husband was out of town on business, and her kids were with a sitter, she found herself in a hotel room with another man. She looked over and saw her reflection in the mirror and that's when reality came rushing back in and she felt as though she could almost hear the devil laughing. Who was this woman she had become?!? She was being driven by a Jezebel spirit of lust. She got dressed, left and cried all the way home. Then the devil started to whisper in her ear…. "You have done so much wrong that God will never forgive you!" "Don't bother praying and trying to make things right, just get divorced and then you can have all the men you want!" "You are worthless! You have defiled yourself and your marriage and God hates you!" Those are the words that ran through her head as the devil tried to keep her on a treadmill of destruction. She longed for comfort which seemed so far away. When she got home she got on her knees and cried and prayed and repented for what seemed like an eternity. She confessed her sin not only to God, but eventually, after nights of crying herself to sleep and a dark depression that started to set in, she confessed to her husband. He left and filed for divorce. For the longest time the devil kept her in his grips with guilt. Even though she was back in church and trying to live right, she felt that if she didn't feel guilty, she wasn't sorry enough; that if she wasn't hurting or suffering, she wasn't being forgiven. And then she met a Christian counselor who told her of God's promises. One who reminded her that God had forgiven her a long time ago, it was now time for her to forgive herself. One who reminded her of the promise in the bible that ALL things are passed away and ALL things become new. That she could draw a line in the sand and move forward and not look back. In fact, she needed to if she were ever going to move forward. Fear, anxiety and doubt are tricks of the devil to keep us from moving forward with the purpose God has for us. It wasn't a quick, easy recovery. She had to work through the loss of the family she had always longed for and envisioned since she was a little girl. She had to work through the shame and the challenges of being a single parent that came with the divorce. Rumors and stares of those who used to hold her in such high regard threatened to keep her bound with guilt and remorse. God had given her one good friend who loved her unconditionally. The one who reminded her that God forgives ALL sins to those with a truly repentant heart. She reminded her that we have all sinned. Unfortunately, some of us sin and the world knows. Others sins stay hidden from the world. But God knows us all and knows our hearts. That's the thing with porn. It may start out as a secret sin, but it's effects often lead to public destruction. Once she made herself right with the Lord again, eventually, things started to look back up. In her darkest moments He would bring that peace that passes all understanding and that would give her the strength for one more day. Now, after her healing, God is using her. She shares her story as she speaks with other young women in an attempt to keep them from heading down the same path of destruction she chose. Her advice to anyone reading this is to stay in the word, pray daily and always guard your heart and mind. Don't open the door for the sin to come in and take your thoughts captive. Thoughts that are dwelled upon will eventually lead to actions.

If you are addicted to pornography, there is power to break those chains of addiction before it destroys your relationships and alters your life. With a truly repentant heart you can find forgiveness as you start a relationship with Jesus, the author of true love.

"The thief comes only to steal and kill and destroy; I have come that they may have life, and have it to the full." – *John 10:10*

CHAPTER 10
LIVING FREE

The purpose of this book from day one, was to help lead people to a life of freedom in Christ Jesus. To give readers the knowledge that you can break the chains that keep you bound in your own personal hell. It's not a twelve step program; it's a one step program. It's not found in a preacher, a denomination or the latest self-help book. It's found by humbling yourself before God and asking for forgiveness. Fear, anxiety, doubt, depression, addiction and un-forgiveness are all tricks of the devil to keep us captive. But there is good news! They have to go in the presence of our Savior. My collaborators and I are believing for great things; but we also know that if just one person finds freedom by finding Jesus through the words written in this book, then we will consider all the time and effort put into it this a total success. If you are that one person and you want to know how to break your chains, continue reading.

You simply have to ask Jesus into your heart and start your own personal relationship with him. It' not about religion, it's about relationship. Salvation is a gift from God. It's not obtained by doing good deeds and being a good person. It can't be earned or bought; it's free to all who accept Jesus into their lives. Ephesians 2 puts it like this:

"Once you were dead because of your disobedience and your many sins. You used to live in sin, just like the rest of the world, obeying the devil – the commander of the powers in the unseen world. He is the spirit at work in the hearts of those who refuse to obey God. All of us used to live that way, following the passionate

desires and inclinations of our sinful nature. By our very nature we were subject to God's anger, just like everyone else. But God is rich in mercy, and he loved us so much, that even though we were dead because of our sins, he gave us life when he raised Christ from the dead. (It is only by God's grace that you have been saved!) For he raised us from the dead along with Christ and seated us with him in the heavenly realms because we are united with Christ Jesus. So God can point to us in all future ages as examples of the incredible wealth of his grace and kindness toward us, as shown in all he has done for us who are united with Christ Jesus.

God saved you by his grace when you believed. And you can't take credit for this; it is a gift from God. Salvation is not a reward for the good things we have done, so none of us can boast about it. For we are God's masterpiece. He has created us anew in Christ Jesus, so we can do the good things he planned for us long ago."

Romans 10 puts it this way:

"The message is the very message about faith that we preach. If you confess with your mouth that Jesus is the Lord and believe in your heart that God raised him from the dead, you will be saved. For it is by believing in your heart that you are made right with God, and it is by confessing with your mouth that you are saved. As the Scriptures tell us, "Anyone who trusts in him will never be disgraced. Jew and Gentile are the same in this respect. They have the same Lord who gives generously to all who call on him. For 'Everyone who calls on the name of the Lord will be saved.' But how can they call on him to save them unless they believe in him? And how can they believe in him if they have never heard about him? And how can they hear about him unless someone tells them? And how will anyone go and tell them without being sent? This is why the Scriptures say, 'How beautiful are the feet of messengers who bring good news!'"

That last line above from Romans is why this book was written. To share the good news that there is hope! As the world gets darker, there is still a light that shines and his name is Jesus. To ask Him into your heart and life, one must have a repentant heart and say the sinners prayer, asking Jesus to come into their lives as Lord and Savior.

The Sinners Prayer: *"Dear Lord Jesus, I know I am a sinner, and I ask for your forgiveness. I believe you died for my sins and rose from the dead. I trust and follow you as my Lord and Savior. Guide my life and help me to do your will. In your name, Amen."*

OK – I've said the prayer - So now what??

Some ask Jesus into their hearts and are set free and immediately delivered from heroin addictions, alcohol, suicide, etc. But it's just the start of their journey. Don't be surprised if you said the sinner's prayer after reading this book and temptation and battles come your way. It's not that you didn't get saved. There is a spiritual battle for your soul. It's kind of like that ex that doesn't want you, until someone else has you. You know the type! When you are living like the world, the devil doesn't bother you. He has you. You're on the highway to hell on your own accord. But once you try to turn around, that's when temptations start to come to try to turn you away from your new relationship with Jesus and the new path you are walking. That's when you have to dig your heels in and say "I will fight the good fight!" Some people view Christians as "wimpy". But I'm here to tell you that this life isn't for the wimpy, whiny or easily discouraged. Staying in sin is easy. You have to lace up your boots and move forward with courage and a holy boldness. You have to be strong enough to stand firm in your belief with a quiet confidence and not be swayed. The good thing is we don't have to do battle with the devil unarmed; you can equip yourself by putting on the whole armor of God.

Ephesians 6:10 – 17 reminds us of this final word from Paul to the church at Ephesus:

A final word: Be strong in the Lord and in his mighty power. Put on all of God's armor so that you will be able to stand firm against all strategies of the devil. For we are not fighting against flesh-and-blood enemies, but against evil rulers and authorities of the unseen world, against mighty powers in this dark world, and against evil spirits in the heavenly places. Therefore, put on every piece of God's armor so you will be able to resist the enemy in the time of evil. Then after the battle, you will still be standing firm. Stand your ground, putting on the belt of truth and the body armor of God's righteousness. For shoes, put on the peace that comes from the Good News so that you will be fully prepared. In addition to all of these, hold up the shield of faith to stop the firey arrows of the devil. Put on salvation as your helmet, and take the sword of the Spirit, which is the word of God.

Indulge me while I dissect that verse just a bit with the things I have learned on my journey:

For shoes, put on the peace that comes from the Good News so that you will be fully prepared. God's Holy Spirit gives us a peace that passes all understanding. Christians deal with the same things everyone else does. Being a Christian doesn't keep us from having trials, but it does change how we deal with them. When it feels like the world is falling down around you and you stand strong on God's promises, reminding yourself of Romans 8:28 "All things must work together for good for those who love the Lord and are called according to his purpose." That's when your faith grows. When you don't let the storm toss you to and fro and instead, rise above the storm. The storm may still be raging, and you should be going crazy inside, but instead there's that peace that surpasses all understanding. The devil resides in fear, anxiety and doubt. So to have peace, you stop his entrance.

He may cause the storm, but he can't reside there if you give him no place.

I have a note in the front of my bible from a sermon by Pastor Darlene. She had us write down a list of our arsenal to fight the good fight:

- The word of God – read your bible
- Power and Authority as a believer to use his name – In the name of Jesus, the enemy has to flee.
- The blood of the lamb has covered us
- Praise – Our praise is a weapon! When we find ourselves in the midst of a storm and instead of giving in to fear, anxiety and doubt we praise, that confuses the devil. We are calling his bluff and calling on our God.
- Testimony – we are saved by the blood of the lamb and the word of our testimony. Tell others about Jesus and what he's done for you. Hearing others testimonies also builds our faith.
- Fasting
- Prayer
- Power of the Holy Spirit
- Angels sent by God for protection
- Power of Agreement between believers – Matthew 18:19
- Whole armor of God
- Love wins every battle – when your emotions tell you to hate and you choose instead to love. The devil doesn't reside in love.
- Knowledge – Don't try to find your knowledge on a YouTube sermon or Google search. Open your bible and pray for God's wisdom as you read.

Satan's only weapon against us is to doubt the word of God. If we stay steadfast in our faith and believing in God's word, we win.

There is power in the words you speak. Speak life, truth and love into every situation and that's what you will have. If you speak negativity, doom, gloom and doubt, that's what you will have. Watch your words closely. Hold every word captive and think about it before it's spoken.

Surround yourself with those on the same journey you are on which may mean deleting some numbers from your phone. If you were delivered from drugs, take the drug dealers out of your contact list; get rid of that temptation. Get plugged in at a good bible-based church that preaches the truth. But most importantly, if you seek God with all your heart, that's where you will find Him.

May God be with you and richly bless you as you start your journey to living free!

Thank You!

I want to sincerely thank you for purchasing this book which has helped plant a seed of hope in Ellie May's Garden! God gave me a vision not too long before the release of this book that I would like to share with you:

Sometimes I feel the nudging to go through the Dunkin Donuts drive-thru where I get my mocha iced coffee, and hand the cashier one of my Ellie May's Garden cards. They hand this card to the driver behind me when they tell that patron their bill was paid for. I always look in the rearview mirror and see who it is God has nudged me to bless that day. I always find myself trying to imagine their story; do they look happy? Sad? Know Jesus? Never heard of Him? Can I get outta there before they get their stuff and realize I paid for it? (Sometimes that's a challenge in the mornings if traffic is heavy. I speed out of there like I just stole the last chocolate covered, sprinkled, glazed donut -trying not to be seen!) One morning last winter I was running late for work, yet something told me to pull in. Later that day, there was a post and picture on the Ellie May's Garden Facebook page and I didn't have to imagine that day's story. The young mother shared how much that random act of kindness had meant to her. She had left her homemade coffee on the roof of her car as she drove off that morning. Someone had been rude to her in the store. She was wondering if anyone even cared anymore... and then she got handed her coffee and the card. When I read that I was so glad I listened to that still small voice. The cool thing about God is that if I hadn't listened, He would've just used someone else to remind her. But man! What an awesome, humbling feeling it is when you're the one He uses!

This particular day I was running late, but got that nudging to pull in the Dunkin Donuts drive-thru, paid for the one behind me, and knew this day would eventually come. $19.97 for the guy behind me! He was obviously very hungry or buying for the office. Smiling, I said to my Dunkin Donut friend, "Ouch! I knew this day would come." We both laughed and she said, "We call you the 'wave maker' here." I said "What?!?" She said "Yep, you always start a wave when you come through. You'll pay for someone's and drive off and then it goes on for the next 8 or 10 cars. It's really kind of cool to experience from in here." That took me by surprise as I had never really thought about anyone other than the person in line right behind me. As I drove off and was processing what she shared, I had this vision instantly come to mind: The similarity between the Dunkin Donuts drive-thru and how I hope heaven is for me. In the wave at the drive-thru, the random act of kindness initiated trickled down the row and people I will never know, or didn't catch a glimpse of in my rear view mirror, were blessed. As I drove away I pictured myself entering a room in heaven and saw those souls I had known and helped. And then I saw a group of souls I'd never seen before in another room. They were waiting to meet and welcome me. One young lady came up to me and said "Because you spoke hope and love into my mom she didn't take her life. She became the mom I needed her to be." A young boy said, "Because my dad read your book he got help for his addiction and was around to be the dad I needed." And there were more waiting to meet me and tell me how while I never knew them, I had still affected their lives through a series of events. That thought hit me like a ton of bricks at 7:15 am as I made my commute towards work. Just a couple of months prior I had a dream where I saw a young boy sitting on bleachers in my old high school gym. He had his head in his hands and was crying. I walked up to him and said "What's wrong?!?" He said "You never told me! Why didn't you ever tell me about Jesus?!?!" I just looked at him in shock and with sadness as I said "I didn't know you?!?!" That dream haunted my thoughts for quite a while as I tried to figure out its meaning. I came to the same conclusion I reached with that day's positive, happy vision. The little boy on the bleachers was symbolic of those opportunities to reach out that were missed. The vision this particular morning, those opportunities pursued. We never know what effects our actions will have on others. Positive or negative, every action has a far-reaching chain reaction. It was a good reminder for me to be sure I'm sowing the right seeds and making the right waves!

Pondering the above vision for a few weeks before the book release, what I already knew in my heart became even more evident. While I want everyone who picks up this book and reads it to have a shift in their life; find hope, freedom, love and be blessed – that's not enough. I don't want it to stop there. If Ellie May's Garden donates a portion of the profit back into missions that are making a difference, even more lives can be affected. Some who may not even read this book, but benefit from it all the same; like those surprise guests I saw in that room in heaven. Thank you once again for purchasing this book and helping Ellie May's Garden fund missions and sow seeds that are making a difference! *Together we CAN make a difference!!*

Much Love and Many Blessings,
Kris

ABOUT THE AUTHOR

Kristina (Kris) Thomas lives in the Cincinnati, OH area where she is employed as a Quality Engineering Specialist. Kris has been in the Aviation industry since 1989. She is also a philanthropist with a passion for writing and outreach ministries. Kris serves as a Court Appointed Special Advocate (CASA) in Clermont County, OH for abused and neglected children in the Child Protective Services system. She has also volunteered at Children's Hospital and was instrumental in starting "Kings Closet" a clothing ministry at Solid Rock Church. She was awarded the "Silver Wings of Excellence" for humanitarian efforts by a previous employer for organizing charity events. Kris believes we are called to be the hands and feet of Jesus; to not just sit in the pews and get filled up, but to fill up so that we can give from the overflow. She loves meeting new people and hearing their stories. When asked once what her dream job would be? She would love to travel, meet new people, write and share their stories. By visiting Ellie May's Garden at www.elliemaysgarden.com (a web-site dedicated to the memory of Kris's mother Eleanor Irvin) you will be connected to Kris's blog.

Resources:

Hope Over Heroin: www.hopeoverheroin.com – website where one can find schedule of events and locations, videos, how to help and ways to donate. You can also find them on the Facebook page - Hope Over Heroin

Mercy Ministries: (women's recovery center) www.mercyministries.com – web site where one can read testimonies, find locations, get help or donate.

Fight the New Drug: www.fightthenewdrug.org – website where one can read stories, statistics and ways to help prevent the harmful effects of pornography addiction.

"Living Free": (Classes for men and women that have suffered physical and mental abuse, anger, depression, suicide or addiction) – these are held at Solid Rock Church (South Campus) every Thursday evening at 6pm. Address: 3946 Hopper Hill Road, Cincinnati, OH 45255.

Cincinnati Restoration Church: (men and women's homes) www.cintirestoration.org – website were one can read testimonies, get contact information and donate.

Darlene Bishop Home for Life: (women's home) www.dbhl.org – website where one can read testimonies, get contact information and donate.

Made in the USA
Columbia, SC
19 August 2018